Dedicated To

The

5th Gold Coast Regt.

"WEST AFRICAN WAY"

The Story of the Burma Campaigns, 1943 - 1945

5TH BN. GOLD COAST REGT.
81 WEST AFRICAN DIVISION

The Naval & Military Press Ltd

Published by
The Naval & Military Press Ltd
5 Riverside, Brambleside, Bellbrook
Industrial Estate, Uckfield, East Sussex,
TN22 1QQ England
Tel: +44 (0) 1825 749494
Fax: +44 (0) 1825 765701
www.naval-military-press.com
www.military-genealogy.com

In reprinting in facsimile from the original, any imperfections are inevitably reproduced and the quality may fall short of modern type and cartographic standards.

FOREWORD

This book is intended to give a general outline of the two campaigns fought in Burma by the 81st West African Division. It has not been compiled from official records and is therefore not historically accurate. In consequence there must also be inaccuracies, and in some cases it may appear unjust or that insufficient justice has been given to various feats and plans. But I simply wished to write a story of what I saw, heard, and felt I knew in order to show as best I could the difficulties under which we fought, and what was in the main achieved. I wanted people to know what the African did rather more than they would in sifting the mass of facts and figures in an official history. I have therefore avoided dates and other figures as far as possible.

Of necessity I have had to base my story on what I saw and experienced with the 5th Battalion Gold Coast Regiment. I loved it and was very proud of it. But I felt that in telling their story I would also be telling the story of all the other units in the Division, which was what I would have liked to do.

The African soldier deserves great honour, and we in this country are more indebted to him than we probably know. He fought with hardly any of the incentives which kept us going, merely believing that what we told him would be true, yet understanding very little of what we told.

I have not been able to do justice to the last part of the second campaign, leading up to the capture of Myohaung, because I was evacuated just prior to that stage.

CONTENTS

GENERAL MAP OF THE THEATRE OF OPERATIONS
FOREWORD

CHAPTER 1	The First West African Division	1	5
CHAPTER 2	"West African Way".	6	10
CHAPTER 3	First Action at Kanwa.	11	14
CHAPTER 4	Mindanywa and Point 13	15	20
CHAPTER 5	The Action at Minthazeik	21	24
CHAPTER 6	"Cox's Corner".	25	33
APPENDIX A	"Long Distance Patrol".		
CHAPTER 7	"The Kyringi Loop"	34	42
CHAPTER 8	Westwards, and the action at Pyingyaung	43	48
CHAPTER 9	Pre-Monsoon.	49	55
CHAPTER 10	Rest, recuperation and Rain.	56	58
CHAPTER 11	Deception.	59	66
APPENDIX B	"On Being Shot-up on Patrol		
CHAPTER 12	Development of a Threat	67	70
CHAPTER 13	Counter-attack at Tinma.	71	75
APPENDIX C	"Xmas Party"		
CHAPTER 14	Final Objective, Myahaung.	76	80
CHAPTER 15	Reflection.	81	84
APPENDIX D	Mileages covered by 5th Gold Coast Regt.		
APPENDIX E	Casualties.		
APPENDIX F	Extracts of Citations of African Awards.		

MAPS

Mindanywa	15
Point 13	18
Minthazeik	22
"Cox's Corner".	27
Pyingyaung	44
Teimagyaung Pya.	62
Yowang and Auklo.	64

CHAPTER I

THE FIRST WEST AFRICAN DIVISION.

THE history, composition and structure of the West African Forces is little known to most people outside the Regular Army and the Colonial Service, and but for short references to their doings in official communiques and on the lesser read pages of the great newspapers, there has been no detailed account of the creditable part that they took in the strenuous Burma campaigns. Even by the end of this great war there will not be many more who know much about the R.W.A.F.F., so it would be a great pity if the brave things they did and the special type of action they carried out was allowed to be forgotten.

The Royal West African Frontier Force had had its beginnings in the armed frontier police forces in the four West African Colonies. All through the later years of the last century it played its role in the inter-tribal wars and in breaking down the last resistance to British rule. Then it rapidly developed into its present form and in the last forty years it has been invaluable in maintaining law and order.

The "Waff" as it was always called, together with the King's African Rifles, was the great stand-by in the British Army for officers seeking adventure, and for those who wanted greater responsibility, good sport, and the means whereby to pay their tailors' bills. The work was easy, the pay was good and the long periods of leave allowed on account of the unhealthy climate there were a great attraction. In such conditions the "Waff" acquired quite a special character of its own, light-hearted perhaps at times--its exploits were often frowned upon by the authorities--but nevertheless with a deep-lying sense of responsibility and an esprit-de-corps quite as high as any other force.

After the East African Campaign in 1940-41 the forces sent there were all returned to the "Coast", and for many long months afterwards it did not seem that there could be any suitable employment for the troops outside their own territory. The fall of France in 1940, and a situation in which the four colonies found themselves surrounded and cut off from each other by a vast Vichy-governed territory, brought about a vast expansion to ensure their security. There was particularly the vital naval and convoy base Freetown to be guarded and the expanding of air bases of Accra and Takoradi, through which a growing stream of British and American aircraft were flowing to our hard pressed forces in the Middle East. It was a dull but essential job. The process was laborious and costly, but for all its magnitude it was completed quickly. It was therefore rather a shock in Decemeber 1942 to find that, with North Africa completely in our hands, there appeared to be no further reason for our existence.

In the long months during which the forces were being patiently built up a considerable amount of training had been carried out, but it was not felt generally in the R.W.A.F.F. that we were fitted to play a part in any likely operations in the future. The greater part of the time had been spent on organization, and re-organization, and any training done was based on the eventuality of small mobile operations, designed to meet and delay attacks from the landward side of each of the four colonies. People therefore felt that our most likely role was that of L. of C. troops in North Africa or labour duties or coastal defence, and that was rather a poor prospect. The G.O.C. West Africa, however, had other ideas. He had been through the East African Campaign during the first World War and he was convinced that it would be possible to train the troops for jungle warfare in Burma. It was through his faith in our ability that we were allotted this role and thus that early in 1943 the 81st West African Division -- the first African Division to be formed--was born.

Before proceeding to the tale of its doings, and more particularly to the story of the 5th Gold Goast Regiment to which I was posted, it is of some interest to show how the expansion took place and with what difficulties we were faced.

All the armed forces on the West Coast, prior to the war, were administered by the Colonial Office and paid for out of the revenues of the Colonies concerned. Rather naturally they were kept to a minimum. There was but one Company in the Gambia, a battalion of two rifle companies in Sierra Leone, two battalions and a mountain battery in the Gold Coast, and but four and a battery in the whole of Nigeria. In addition there was a territorial battalion in the Gold Coast about whose doings this story mainly deals. Beyond these few units there was nothing else. There were no military hospitals, no pay services or supply depots, no engineers or signals and but mere skeletons of Headquarters, while the coastal defence batteries were obsolete and out of use. The African soldier fed himself out of his pay, and his clothing and equipment was provided through the Crown Agents for the Colonies, The Officers and British N.C.Os were found from British Regiments and they were normally under establishment.

Shortly before the war the G.O.C, West Africa, General Sir George Giffard, obviously succeeded in persuading the Government that urgent steps were necessary to ensure the expansion of the R.W.A.F.F., should it be necessary. One of his first steps was to make an arrangement whereby the Rhodesia Regiment should supply a large number of Officers and N.C.Os to increase establishment on the outbreak of war, and their prompt arrival in 1939 made the initial expansion possible. The Coastal Defences were also put in hand, but this caused a considerable drain on the existing resources of the African N.C.Os which the subsequent expansion made it even more difficult to make up.

As soon as war broke out it became obvious that administration by the Colonial Office was out of the question, so it was only then that the War Office began to take over the system of supply. Headquarters sprang up and around them transport services, ordinance, pay offices and movements, signal services and hospitals. Except for the key personnel, the majority recruited for all these were Africans and, as can be imagined, the drain on the supply of the educated types required was very considerable. If the demand had been confined only to the Army it would have been a comparatively simple matter, but at the same time there were similar demands for motor drivers, clerks, labourers and medical orderlies by the Government, the Navy and the R.A.F. While the R.W.A.F.F. were doubling and trebling their numbers there were also aerodromes, roads and defence works to be built and all these called for huge camps which never seemed to keep pace with the urgent demands for accommodation.

It is hardly surprising therefore that over a long period from 1940 the West African Forces were little more than a large elementary training organization. In my own unit in Sierra Leone we had to find N.C.O's for three new units within a period of about eight months, and of course it became necessary to train the replacements for these before any real progress could be made in the private soldier category. Likewise the recruits seemed to keep slipping through our fingers for a very long time. In peace time they were not considered of very much value in under a year, but now some of them were required as N.C.O's in much less than that time.

Officers and British N.C.O's also presented many difficulties. It takes a good and experienced officer to make a success of his command over African troops, and yet many of those we received were naturally almost straight from Officer's Training Units. Their sickness rate was very high, mainly on account of malaria, and with the usual high number of incompatibles, who had to be returned to their British units, it was difficult to achieve any real stability for a long time. The whole thing was aggravated in the matter of Europeans because almost from first to last the majority of them felt convinced that nothing would ever be done with the R.W.A.F.F., and their main desire was to get back to British service as soon as possible.

There were also constant changes of establishment, which might be expected in any force growing so rapidly; constant movements to meet an ever changing situation, and always, because we were such a low-priority force, a shortage of weapons, clothing and equipment.

By the middle of 1942, however, the task was almost complete. There were new Coast Defences then along the entire coast between Freetown and Lagos. Freetown, in addition, simply bristled with anti-aircraft batteries. Great airfields had sprung up from Takoradi to the Middle East. There were military hospitals in every big military centre, as well as training schools and rest camps. Every unit had its full complement of motor vehicles and the drivers trained for them - where not one had existed before 1940. All the technicians, which are required by any modern force, had been supplied and trained out of the slender resources of a backward tropical people.

It was a fine achievement and must undoubtedly be largely attributed to the foresight of General Giffard who had studied the whole problem shortly before the war began.

It ought to be realized that the average African can by no means be described as a natural warrior. First and foremost he is a farmer, who is lucky in that he has to do very little work in the fertile soil in order to lead a very happy and comfortable existence. He is therefore cheerful, kind and peaceable, and he has been so well looked after that there has been no reason for him to indulge in quarrels and inter-tribal strife for a very long time.

The African is much more interested in the pageant of soldiering than its more practical application, and the average man is totally unaware of the violence and strife which can go on in the outside world, or of the possibility of its affecting him in any way. So it was an uphill job to train the much lower standard of recruit who had to be called up during the war. Most of them, by African standards, were slow and under-nourished, and the language difficulty, on account of the high percentage of new officers, was considerable. But it was mainly in explaining to him the meaning of the present war, and the righteousness of his taking part in it that our greatest problems arose. We could be sure of his loyalty and obedience when subjected to the most strenuous tasks, but could we expect him to follow us in action unless he felt that there was a cause which compelled him to do his uttermost? I am inclined to doubt that we ever succeeded. His imagination simply would not run to it. Fortunately his belief in the officer's word was so strong that it proved sufficient to carry him through the greatest trials.

So it was that by April 1943 the units which were to make up the 81st West African Division came at length to be concentrated in Nigeria for their preliminary battle training. From Sierra Leone came the 4th Nigerians, the 1st Sierra Leone and the 1st Gambia Battalions; from the Gold Coast came the 5th, 7th and 8th Gold Coast, and in Nigeria already were the 6th, 7th and 12th Nigerians. These groups made up the 6th, 5th and 3rd Brigades respectively, and over them Major General Woolner C.B., M.C., was given command.

It was not a propitious time of year for concentrated training to begin, for the heavy rains were just about to start, but it was a perfect preparation for the hardships which were to follow. We were despatched almost immediately on arrival to an area of virgin bush, where the towering cotton trees shut out the light. This was to be our camp - "get on with it," we were told; "make yourselves comfortable as best you can".

We succeeded pretty well. In the damp undergrowth we hacked and cleared away the space for our living accommodation, dug the drains, repaired the road, cleared parade grounds and even football fields, and constructed our own ranges and assault courses. A maze of small paths, two or three feet wide, connected up each hidden platoon and company area, and were it not for the day-long sounds of rifle fire and bursting grenades it would have been possible to drive past the area without ever being aware that it was a battalion camp.

Our Battalion, 5th Gold Coast, was full of recruits and the training done could only be elementary. A powerful effort was made to perfect a jungle battle drill while we were there, but we found in practice that it turned out to be a failure, for the African only learns what he is being taught at the moment, and he sees no connection with drill movements on the parade ground and the fluidity of future action. As a result a good deal of precious time was wasted, though not completely so, because the drill movements that he did at least taught him to react quickly to situations and words of command. But a golden opportunity was lost, in the thick bush of Southern Nigeria to practise the individuality and cunning of the jungle fighter and to discover the difficulties of control and the dangers of surprise. By concentrating on automatic action, the opportunity was lost for planning and the issue of clear-cut orders.

We lived and trained in intervals of torrential rain and steamy sunshine, filtering through the great trees above us. It was a very brief preparation, but nevertheless quite a valuable period. A spirit of enthusiasm grew up in every unit which, I think, any Divisional Commander might pride himself, and in a fury of hard work the few weeks passed quickly by with their hardships scarcely noticed. By the end of August, only about four months after it had been formed, the Division sailed for India, and in September they were in camp once again with an even shorter time in front of them before they were sent in to action.

It did not dismay us, but it certainly seemed that a period of only two further months training in a new country was about as short as anyone could be asked to do. Making allowance for the periods spent in the disposal and preparation of camps before and after our various moves, and for the period of the voyage, it meant that we should have had about four and a half months available for training since the formation of the division.

Our arrival in India was not auspicious. As we crept along dusty roads in the falling twilight a huge white encampment spread itself before us. It had many buildings to be seen, though few of them had roofs on; and many labourers, but few of them working. There were several road traces, but that was as far as the roads had got; a steamroller stood silent without steam; and many tents were there but it was obvious that we should have to pitch most of them. We discovered a canteen, but it hardly seemed likely that its two small tents would suffice for six thousand men. Finally it was raining gently and there was mud, thick and unpleasant, everywhere.

Nevertheless our brief stay at Nazik was by no means an unhappy period. The camp was set in a huge plain high up in the Western Ghats and - arriving as we did at the tail end of the monsoon - the whole countryside was a brilliant mixture of green and brown, splashed with great patches of brilliant yellow flowers. Around us abrupt, curiously shaped hills, often bearing no relation to each other, leapt upwards from the faintly undulating fields, and on many of them were quaint Hindu temples cut out of the rock, a constant reminder of the sanctity in which this area is held. The sun was very hot for most of the day, but at night it was a luxury to be able to use blankets again, and the crisp morning air was a bribe to be up and doing. Here we were back again to clubs and cinemas after an interval of many months, and to newspapers only a day old. There was a queer local whisky to become acquainted with and always the possibility of a visit to Bombay.

With a campaign so close upon us, it would have been easy to embark on ambitious schemes of training but most improbable that they would have been carried out. It so often happens in the Army: in striving to attain to perfection, next to nothing is eventually achieved. But we were not ambitious. Finding that the time available was far less than we had expected, we set out to master the bare essentials of jungle warfare - to endure long marches, to maintain control over the immensely long columns which are so characteristic of this type of country, and to "harbour" ourselves before dark.

The principles of habouring, as we learnt them, were reminiscent of Wellington's squares. It was possible in them to bring fire to bear in any direction. Each unit and sub-unit had its own reserves, while the Headquarters and administrative personnel occupied the centre. The idea we followed was that normal co-ordinated defence was impossible in such blind country, and that therefore the best form of action was to hide away completely at night so that it was unlikely that we should be attacked at all. It was very important that we should master this technique, because we were particularly vulnerable on account of the large percentage of unarmed carriers in each unit.

Such an idea seemed simple enough; but it was quite a different matter when we came to put it into action. It is not so easy to select a piece of ground when a move of only a few yards right or left causes you to lose sight entirely of the ground you started on.

It is difficult to estimate its size when the nature of the ground and the tangled undergrowth prevents you taking any two consecutive steps of the same length. Also the effort to cut out the various connecting paths to company areas, so easily shown on a diagram, seemed at first a hopeless puzzle. The economic size of advance parties was also a matter of much trial and error while, whereas the reconnaissance officer might manage well enough to select his company areas, he often found it very difficult to get back to the place where he started.

It seems strange to look back now - when harbouring is the simplest problem - on all these difficulties: the angry protests when insufficient space was allowed and areas overlapped; the traffic blocks; the points of detail forgotten; the noise and the discomfort and the deadly slowness of it all, while feet ached and tired minds longed for a cup of tea. But in the two brief months at Nazik we managed to master what we had set out to do. We became hard and fit, and in its final test the whole Brigade completed a four day's march in mountainous country in single file - a column many miles long. Such an operation requires much staff work and very good judgment by every junior commander, but until it can be done without check or fuss it is practically impossible to operate a force in dense jungle country. We learnt little enough, but that was about all there was time to do.

So the day quickly came along when we had to embark on our final operations - the last check of every item of equipment, the final discarding of every unnecessary thing; the completion of wills, the sorting out of documents and the issue of maps. We paid the last bills, watched the storage of all our most personal comforts, and clung to the last stick of furniture until it could be held no longer...... Then we were ready.

Within only six months or our formation as a division in West Africa we entrained for Calcutta and ten days later arrived in Chittagong, the entrance to the Arakan.

CHAPTER II

"WEST AFRICAN WAY"

THE lower Kaladan Valley and the long, narrow area of the coast from north of Chittagong to south of Akyab is the great rice producing area of the Arakan. The coastal belt is not pleasing country. For miles on either side of the only road, which had to be constructed to carry supplies to the main forces of XV Corps, the ground stretches bare and absolutely flat on one side to the sea, on the other to the hazy Arakan Yomas. The land is sallow. Parched paddy fields, on which the slightest movement raises a cloud of dirty grey dust, extend as far as the eye can see. Small clusters of drab bamboo huts, grass-roofed, do nothing to break the monotony, and the heavy, dark green mango trees among them - solid and utterly still - seem to add a stifling effect to the whole atmosphere. The flat ground is a tangle of water courses which wander, bewildered, till they find some small depression in which to come to rest. Parched in the hot weather, except for the many "tanks" constructed to preserve the water supplies, the land is transformed in the monsoon into as great an expanse of water - a dreary flood. Only when the brilliant green rice seedlings are planted, or before the crops ripen, is there any attraction to be found there.

It was along the axis of this one road that the British forces in Arakan fought their way southwards in 1942 - 1943 to within striking distance of Akyab, only to be driven back because their resources were too weak to resist the inevitable counter - threat to their own communications. Now at the end of 1943, with more experience and rather better material, the effort was to be made again. This time however it was hoped - by means of a diversion in the Kaladan Valley and by an amphibious operation later in the campaign - that the objective, Akyab, could at last be reached.

The choice of our West African division for the operations in the Kaladan was an obvious one. To get there entailed a march of more than 70 miles over some of the wildest country imaginable. Any force attempting it, therefore, would have to be very mobile and also capable of operating with a minimum of transport, or even without transport at all. This was our meat, for men - poor creatures - can get anywhere, and with us the majority of our baggage was carried on men's heads. Thus it came about that early in December, in the morning sunlight, our battalion could be seen, strung out across the paddy fields, on its first march towards the grey-blue hills which separated them from the Kaladan Valley.

The maps issued to us were large scale maps and quite sufficient to indicate that we must be prepared for something which none of us had experienced before. The country was formidable. It was largely without form. For the first part our route followed the course of the Matamahari River, through villages which will never be shown on the most expensive atlas. Later - and this was not yet decided - it must find its way from one valley over mountains into the next, and then again over three precipitous and ever greater ridges before it fell down to the banks of the Kaladan river. When we had seen the nature of these tasks the intermediate ones seemed hardly worth consideration, but even they would have seemed formidable to troops operating in easier country.

There were tracks marked here and there over these turbulent contours, but to anyone with even the most elementary knowledge of map reading it was obvious that they represented little else than the paths normally followed by the hill people, visiting one village or another. There could be no regular route here between India and Burma, because the fierce monsoon rains yearly washed the tracks away, changing the faces of the hillsides and transforming the river-bed routes into roaring torrents of muddy water. Somewhere about half-way the formidable barrier of "Frontier Ridge" lay across our path, in some places nearly two thousand feet high, rocky and precipitous, and with but two or three places through which even the natives thought it fit to pass; while in the same area we noticed that the rivers fought their way to north, south, east and west, a perfect nightmare of cartography.

His project was not viewed very hopefully by the authorities, but through this piece of country the Divisional Commander decided that it would be possible to build a road, capable of taking jeeps and 30-cwt lorries. There had been some discussion as to whether the force should move entirely without transport, and this was the way we eventually came to operate, but it was not considered entirely practicable at the time. Provided a road could be made, the guns and heavy signal equipment were to be carried in M.T.

After one look at the map, nobody in the division really felt the feat was possible. But the General himself was a Sapper. He had discovered that the hills were composed almost entirely of sand and clay and therefore felt certain that some way over could be found. The story goes that the C.R.E. became equally convinced that there was none, and that an amusing exchange of telegrams took place.

"Further progress impossible" wired the C.R.E., or words to that effect, after the most extensive reconnaissance of the surrounding country.

"Proceed", replied the General, "or take the next boat home". Whereon the Sappers tried again, but with no further success. So, convinced that he was right, another wire was sent. It was no good "Please book passage", he wrote.

The answer to which was simply - "No"!

The C.R.E., of course, found a way in the end. He had to. And it was now to be our task to assist in its construction as we marched eastwards along the banks of the Matamahari River.

A four day's struggle to the village of Amtoli brought us to the area where the work was to begin. The greater part of the way had been along the banks of the river, but the few hills which we *had* passed over were so steep that, in our innocence, we imagined nothing worse could befall us. The first day after our arrival was destined for our disillusionment.

Soon after dawn the two leading companies set off through the river mists to their working areas, several miles up the river. "If you don't want to walk in water all the way", someone advised, "I should take the short cut over the hills". He pointed to mountain in front. "It's a bit rough", he added. "We call it the 'Hill of a Thousand Steps'". Two hours later we agreed. It was rough. And there were, very probably, a thousand steps.

It was our first experience of a real Burma hill - the type where you gasp your way to the summit, only to find, just round the corner, that it still stretches upwards, a long way out of reach. The pace is a crawl; the column checks, goes on a few paces and checks again; carriers groan under their heavy loads; and tired reluctant Europeans trace and re-trace their steps along the column trying to keep things moving. Two-thirds of the way through this march the hill fell down again abruptly to the river, but that offered little relief. It was so steep in one part that each load had to be lowered on rifle slings for the first thirty feet, and thereafter the effort to prevent one-self going too fast down the slippery path was about as tiring as the climb. Thereafter the river route was used.

For some twenty miles of more, the trace of the road followed for the most part, the course of the Tuin Khiang, a rocky stream on the average about thirty yards wide. It was possible for loaded jeeps to drive for appreciable distances along the river bed as it existed, casting backwards and forwards to a strip of dry ground, first on one bank and then on the other. But from then on the hills closed right in, rising up almost sheer from the banks, and there were long stretches where they had to be cut away, or where the deeper parts of the river had to be filled up laboriously by hand with stones. It meant long hours standing in the water or trudging wearily through it for literally miles at a time, and it was exhausting work. There were no mechanical aids - no bulldozers or mechanical drills: the pick, shovel and a stick of gelignite were our only tools.

Right forward to the Kaladan, in little camps among the hills, there were battalions alloted to the various sectors, and as a job was completed, either a company or the whole unit would leap-frog forward to the next task. In between them, the Auxiliary Group companies (our supply organization) who may be thought of as human lorries, ferried supplies ceaselessly backwards and forwards sweating over the most appalling gradients, or wet through to the waist through rivers.

The work in the rivers was unpleasant but comparatively easy. The worst thing about it was the difficulty in ever getting dry, for the mists blotted out the hills early in the evening and clung to the river beds often until after ten o'clock in the morning. There were many places, however, where, on account of the waterfalls or deep water, it was necessary to divert over the mountains, and here the work was difficult and a real labour. There were many big rocks which had laboriously to be just picked away, and great banks to be constructed merely from the earth carried by the men in small baskets on their heads.

It was a race against time, for a serious outbreak of cholera prevented any movement up and down the road for several days. Christmas passed by on a diet of "bully" and biscuits and a shortage of cigarettes, but it was hardly noticed. Each day the target date drew closer and the completion of the task was all that mattered.

As the road took shape it became somehow alive and worked up our enthusiasm. It was one day just a task, and the next -- none knew quite how -- "West African Way." Something entirely our own. Nobody referred to maps, for there were names everywhere, and everybody seemed to know them: "Cox's Causeway," "Bailey's Bridge," "Painter's Pride," "The Waterfall." Further ahead was "Rest and Be Thankful," "Nino" and "Leingthan Hill." All along it were direction signs and notices, facetious or practical -- "Tokyo 3,000"; "Jeepers, right -- Creepers left"; "not far now"; or, quite reasonably for the dangerous downgrade of Leingthan Hill, "Be *BLOODY* Careful"! Somehow every crude and ridiculous notice seemed to have been placed at the spot where a tired man's sense of humour as he struggled despairingly up a never-ending slope, had sunk to its very lowest ebb, reviving him just enough to enable him to stagger over the top.

At length the day came when the 5th Gold Coast had completed their own task, and the real march forward began. Looking back on the daily marches, it is almost impossible to bring imagination to endure again the exhaustion brought about by those hills. One can only remember incidents -- not feelings: the irritation of scrabbling for a foothold on the slippery road, before the morning mists had thinned away; the vexed relief over dip down because it must lead to a further climb; trying to keep the eyes fixed to avoid looking too soon for the top of a hill; even feeling an impersonal sympathy for one's own muscles.

Sometimes the length of pace was so short, and the rate of movement so slow and uneven that one was astonished to discover the rate of progress we actually made on the map. But there was only one pace - that was the slowest which would keep you moving. The essential was that you *should* keep moving - and a check was the signal for recrimination and bad temper along the whole column.

Keep moving! Because one was compelled to keep the mind a blank or keep it filled with any thought or problem which might divert it from physical consideration, it was not very easy to observe the country we passed through. Yet there were impressions which could not be held away. Very often you could walk for miles along the narrow road, shut in all the way by a still and silent wall of bamboo on either side. All that you might see on the flat pieces, which were the only areas you were likely to notice, was the brown carpet of dead leaf falling sharply away on either side. This was on the knife-edged ridges, the only part of a hill along which a road could easily follow. From them the road might suddenly tumble down into a chaung below, much like any Scottish mountain stream, with its smooth boulders of every size, its rocky ledges and clear pools, but shut in completely by trees among the eternal bomboo; and with ferns, creeper and rotting vegetation making solid the space beneath. We welcomed the chaungs only because they were cooler, for otherwise they were difficult and dangerous places for headloaders, and there was also something of the sinister in the stillness which hedged them in on either side. Their innumerable tributaries made map-reading very uncertain, and their twists and turns gave an overated impression of the distance travelled.

If you were lucky you might sometimes halt at the summit of a hill higher than the surrounding country, and then only was it possible to appreciate the wild beauty that lay about. Then the impression was of a coverlet of ivy green, billowed in confusion as far as the eye could reach. For miles every hill lay softened under its bamboo covering, yet still revealed in its wild strength, like muscles in repose beneath the skin of some giant torso. Mile upon mile of tumbled, solid green lay stretched before you, utterly still and completely peaceful under the warm sun. Sometimes across the sharp valleys a troop of monkeys would set up a babel of childish hoots and shrieks which filled the hills with their echoes, but apart from that there was not a wisp of smoke nor a sign of life. In the early mornings the higher peaks pointed upwards from the dense white mists which, as the sun came up, swirled down and up and back again, as if unwillingly to uncover their wild resting place. They soon dispersed, but in the big river valleys the blanket obstinately remained till the sun was high in the sky.

The grandeur of the scene is difficult to describe. It gave the impression mainly of something asleep-peaceful, yet dangerous to disturb. Veined with its multitude of silent streams, their courses merely to be guessed at, it also gave the feeling of secret life stirring just beneath the surface; of millions of germs and microbes essential to life and change. It was not hostile or creepy, but detached and aloof, permitting puny man to pursue his way there if he was strong enough to do so.

We made forced marches. Shivering in the dawn mists, the harbour parties would collect on the track an hour before the main body. As a small party, they could expect to gain a further hour during the course of the march, and the pattern of a new harbour would be complete before the main body arrived. Water points would be marked, firewood cut and the tea boiled and ready. Each section would be guided to its place. The main column, stretched in open file over three thousand yards of road set off at 0730 hours, and on several occasions the last man had not come in before darkness was falling. The average speed was little over a mile an hour.

It is not easy to remember much. There was a hill west of Mawdok where we waited thankfully while empty jeeps charged perilously at a slippery gradient on the turn, skidding wildly and sliding back, beaten, to the foot of it, where engineers patiently flung more stones into the deepening mud to give them a purchase. It takes a good hill to beat a jeep. Then there was Frontier Hill, where even the best map readers, wishfully-thinking, declared at three downgrades that we must have reached the top; yet we found there was a further twenty minutes climb before the triumphal arch was reached with its sign-posts: "Calcutta 500 - Tokyo 3,000."

In one place the smaller headloaders crossed a stream with the racing waters up to their armpits, while officers offered unspoken prayers for the safety of the more precious loads. We set foot at the bottom of an already famous hill - to us - and wondered who the big sissys were who had shot such a line about it. But an hour and a half later, before we had reached the top, we were mentally making our apologies. "Rest and Be Thankful." There the notice was crudely scrawled on a bully-beef box at the summit, and gladly obeyed and stole an unauthorized halt. Calves and thighs ached, temples throbbed, and we could conjure no pity in our tired state for the hundreds of men we knew were still toiling up behind us.

That day was perhaps the worst march we did, for no sooner had we cleared "Rest and Be Thankful" than Nino Hill towered up before us. We had to go down before we could go up. The road tumbled. In a few short minutes all the effort we had made was undone and then an even fiercer climb began. In silence we crawled to the top and by then we were too far gone to appreciate the long descent to Tukpui on the other side.

Finally there was "Leingthan." The ascent there was bad, but the descent was memorable. It was so steep that normal walking was almost impossible, and no jeep could return over it under its own power. For much more than a thousand feet we just slithered the whole way. "Be *BLOODY* careful" - the only possible wording - was the notice posted there, but it was purely formal in reality: there was nothing really that footslogger or driver could do about it.

But these marches, nevertheless, were the almost value to all of us. By the end of them we were as fit and hard as it was possible to be, while we had also gained invaluable experience. Perhaps the most important thing of all in warfare in this frightful country was the ability to be able to move economically. A staff officer's miscalculation in a march table might mean a complete blockage of the only available track; the correct time of start could mean the difference between a hot meal or going hungry; a late arrival at some new harbour might spell disaster through inability to secure the position. It was essential, where the difference in time between the first and last man in the battalion striking camp was as much as ninety minutes, that control and timing should move like clockwork. And all these problems were solved during this period.

At last the day came when from the top of the last great hill we paused to look down to where the dissolving mists revealed a clear, blue river. This was the Kaladan, and it was a big moment for those whose imagination might run to what lay before us. What was in store for us among those broken hills and deep and silent valleys?

Between December 7th 1943, when the 4th Nigerians had left Chiringa, and January 17th nearly the whole Division had been concentrated at their starting point, and the 73 miles of West African Way completed without a mechanical tool of any kind. It was no Ledo Road. Even by now it will probably have disappeared in the jungle undergrowth. But we defeated Nature at the time and for that reason those of us who made it will look back on the feat with much pride.

CHAPTER III

FIRST ACTION AT KANWA

THE little village of Balaing, where we came out on the waters of the Kaladan, was a very important milestone on the long march we were to make through Burma, for it marked the end of West African Way and was also the first place where the Battalion received its supplies by air. It was here too that we first received orders directly concerned with operations. From now on the whole of our large force, numbering nearly 20,000 men, was to be wholly supplied by air, a thing which had never been attempted over an extended period before.

It was a beautiful area. The river here run blue and clear as crystal, curving between sharp hills which dropped down into the water without a check. A mile above the place where we came out on to the river bank the hills fell back a little to the west, leaving a sharp turning circle for the long and narrow beach on which the drop was to take place. It did not seem an easy area in which to manoeuvre large aircraft. Opposite the beach was a small bamboo village, perched on a shelf and within a cleft which was the only break in the cliff running the whole length of the river that side. Behind us the ground was open and fairly flat for a few hundred yards, but then the hills closed in once again and the river took a steep bend to the north east. A slight error in this bumpy atmosphere could easily spell disaster.

We discovered a great feeling of comfort and superiority in being supplied by air. Cut off as we were, even now, by a minimum of ten days marching from the nearest supporting troops, the tuneful hum of the big Dakotas in the distance was a constant reminder that we were not forgotten, and with their support we had no need to worry about our flanks or rear, for our L. of C. was now the sky.

Any air-drop is a beautiful sight. First the Hurricanes appear with a sort of "who - dares" look about them, as in pairs they sweep in opposing circles around the dropping site. The Dakotas are there, shaving over the bamboo hill-tops, dipping down to the site for the O. K. signal, and then away on their anti-clockwise run for the drop to begin.

I shall always remember that first morning, watching it all from the shadows of the opposite bank — the peaceful river, the swelling and receding roar of the aircraft, the emerald hillsides with the white parachutes billowing and floating gently to the ground. In would come each Dakota, banking perilously inside the ring of the surrounding hills, dipping to throw out its loads between the white aiming marks and then-with throttles open wide-rising again to follow the sharp curve of the river bend like a great gull in a stiff sea breeze.

In an hour the drop is over: the Hurricanes make their last friendly sweep, and then suddenly the sky is empty save for the droning of the planes in their quick run for base. There is something dreamlike in the calm that follows, but there lie the parachutes - to show that it was real - scattered along the shore or hanging from the trees, and already hundreds of little black figures are unfastening the cords and carrying the loads on their heads to the supply dump.

After only a day in which to sort ourselves out and distribute the rations, we received orders to resume the march. Far to the south of us we knew that Kyauktaw, where the Kaladan begins to flow slightly westwards towards the sea, was our main objective. Akyab was then only possibility in our minds, and the immediate future and what it held for us was quite obscure. The hill people had informed us that the Japs were concentrated near Paletwa, only a few miles further south, but we were as yet uncertain whether to trust their reports or not. They seemed to us so reserved and furtive, and knowing that many of them had been forced to work for the Japs we were uncertain how to distinguish friend from foe. Because the east bank of the Kaladan was the better going the jeep track had been continued on that side, and the 6th Brigade had been detailed to push it forward. Our battalion was to follow to protect their flank and rear, while the remainder of 5th Brigade moved along the west bank so that the two main forces could converge on Paletwa from east and west.

This period was perhaps the most pleasant of the whole campaign. Previously it had been bitterly damp and cool at night, but now it was cold and fresh and we were marching with the grain of the country. No longer were there any heartbreak hills to climb - Painter's Pride, Nino, Leingthan and Rest and Be Thankful were things of past - and our way led through shady woods with little of the stifling undergrowth which hitherto we had experienced. The marches were short and there was a growing excitement within us which hurried us forward.

We had not long to wait for news. Soon after leaving Balaing the information filtered back that the first contact had been made and the opposition brushed aside. It had only been a standing patrol and so not surprising, but it *was* extraordinary that two of the Japanese had given themselves up without a struggle - a quite unheard - of thing. Corps Headquarters could not believe the message when it was first received.

The appearance of the two prisoners was a great event for the troops, who are intensely interested in people and how they behave, and it was also the occasion for an amusing display of pretended ferocity. The news that the prisoners were passing through the harbour was the signal for a whooping rush with brandished matchets towards the unfortunate pair. "Let me take his ear, Sir!" was a typical remark. It did the troops good though, for I really believe that they had begun to think there would be no action at all. From then on there was far better security at night. Later as we marched on we came upon the trampled elephant grass at the scene of the first action. Then came news through that the Japs were standing to fight at Kanwa and we hurried forward to take up our allotted role.

To those of us who had not been in action before it was a moment of great interest to come up with some of those who had; but we found that imagination was more dramatic than reality. There was nothing unusual about the "Gambias" when we met them, bathing in the river as cheerfully as if they were on holiday. The area was a mass of gleaming black bodies, splashing in the water and laughing and talking in the sunshine. But there was a greater atmosphere of urgency as we went on, and we were passed and repassed by hundreds of hurrying carriers with loads of food and ammunition on their heads. We came across signallers by the track laying cable, and jeeps scrambled past us on urgent errands. At last we halted near 6th Brigade Headquarters, hidden among the trees round a corner and I was sent ahead through the busy area to find the Brigade Major and receive orders.

Sipalaung was the name of the place near which "Brigade" had been set up. Just beyond it lay the Kaladan, running due east from Paletwa and then curving round it sharply to the south. It was a little below this elbow on the western bank that the enemy had taken up the first position which they were prepared to hold against us. This was Kanwa which stood astride the one fair track running south; a formidable position, for it lay among very broken grounds, hidden in the dense undergrowth which normally surrounds deserted Burmese villages, from which there were many spurs rising steeply up from the river bank to a great hill over 1,200 feet high.

The eventual failure to make the best of "Kanwa" was mainly due to over-confidence on our part. When 4 N. R made contact to the north of it they set out to hold the Japs in front, while the remainder of the battalion carried out a most excellent night march over the trackless mountain, to come down in the enemy's rear. They had to cut through the jungle for every yard of the way. Theoretically, therefore, the Japs were surrounded and it was merely a matter of time till they were wiped out. But the result did not work out as expected. Supported by the mortar fire of 1st Sierra Leone from the east bank, they attacked very vigorously from the front, but up the precipitous slopes on top of which nearly all the Japs posts were located their progress was very slow. It was not possible in the time available to get close enough to locate their machine-guns accurately and so to direct the mortar fire on to them. As the time slipped by, it began to be evident that the supply problem for the force in rear had been calculated on the probability of a ready success rather than a long drawn out battle. Adjustments had to be made and in the process the Japs slipped away, unharmed, in small parties over the hills.

If a far greater force had been used to block the exists, and if the R. A. F. had been called in to plaster the area with cannon fire and high explosive prior to the attack, the tale might have been a very different one. It was a pity. However insignificant it might have been, the first Jap force encountered might have been destroyed, and the Division would have gone forward to its next battles after a very heartening beginning.

Immediately on arrival during the battle, 5th Gold Coast were sent off to Konwei where we were to protect the left flank of the 6th Brigade. There our job was to patrol deeply to the east, where a strong force of Japanese had been reported, so we set off to the place with high expectations. It turned out, however, on this occasion - and it was not often the case - that our local information was wrong, so we eventually settle down there to a few more days of quiet before our real labours began.

Konwei was a peaceful place, even within the sound of firing. The chaung there was broad and lazy, trickling among islands of shingle and rounded grey rocks. In quite a small area there were as many as four of the quaint bamboo villages, made everywhere in these part, one poised on an open bluff above the river bank, the others nestled into the hillsides among big trees which run along the river. There were fat cows grazing in the paddy fields, and chickens and a pig or two exploring the green tobacco gardens at the place we chose. The woods were open and shady, and on the steep hillsides you could see the tiny bamboo huts - always on stilts - where the mountain rice is stored during harvest. Blue smoke curled up into the air and a few old men, dignified and solemn, came out to greet us on our arrival.

Our hold-up was necessary because the jeep track had to be continued inland from here, and there were also units who had yet to catch up the forward troops. It was also decided to construct the first "moth-strip" here, a task which was alloted to us, and to build a number of bamboo rafts which were required for carrying stores down the Kaladan. The first job was work we understood, but it must be admitted that raft building was not our strong point. Several of our "efforts" sank slowly and with maddening deliberation as soon as they were launched, and the pride of our fleet, a monster affair, without doubt proudly remained in its fitting out basin until the rains made the river deep enough for it to move out.

The airstrip was completed in four days with only picks and shovels, matchets and crowbars. It was not a bad effort considering that something like a hundred trees had to be removed and that the R.A.F. consistently preferred to use it as their dropping-site instead of the one chosen for them, bombarding us with hundreds of parachutes and loose bags of grain. It was here, I think that we received our first good mail drop, the most important to us of all the necessities which were showered upon us. From then on it was very regular and there were remarkably few losses, while the time taken from England was steadily reduced from something over two weeks to seven days or less. After seeing at first hand the truly remarkable effect it had on our morale and the equally deep depression that was caused if it was felt that the slightest thing had gone wrong, one would place this nearly first in all the important administrative matters which have to be attended to for a force in action. Sugar we found was almost equally important in our simplified existence, for what was an Army cup of tea without sugar, and what is an Army without tea?

It was an event to witness the landing of the first moth in the jungle and to meet someone who an hour ago had moved in a different world. Our policy was to build mothstrips as we went along, evacuating the wounded from them and receiving and sending out important dispatches. Later on we were also to build several fullsized runways so that big Dakotas could take on the job. We watched them enviously sometimes as some neat person in shoes and wearing no equipment stepped out, or when a friend was whisked off into the distance, but on the whole they were no more than just another part of the great machine, as we were. There was a distinctly pleasant side to our existence, though it may be some years before many admit it, and many of us preferred to be hidden away in the Burma valleys rather than to endure desert sand or the mud and slush of continental warfare.

The continuation of the jeep track was pushed on rapidly, and we soon received orders to follow for a short way in the wake of 6th Brigade and then rejoin our own on the west bank of the river Themawa. There was no action, but always slight tension in rounding a corner, which never left us as long as we were in the jungle, or when poking about the deserted villages we passed through.

Following narrow stream beds we arrived in two days once more upon the banks of the Kaladan. We did not quite know how we were going to manage the crossing, for the "I" reports all maintained that the Japs had swept the river bare of every usable canoe, but we had hopes in an officer by the name Hale, who had been sent ahead to do what he could. Hale might not have a very extensive military knowledge, we felt, but where it had ever been a matter of getting anything for us, or of swelling the Regimental Funds, he had never failed us; a small matter of canoes should therefore present no difficulties to him. Sure enough a fleet was there when we arrived, usable but rather the worse for wear. The pioneers were repairing the last hole in one of their canoes with a piece of shirt-tail and some tin as we came down to the beach, and all the others had been similarly patched. They would be all right, he told us cheerfully, provided we bailed out quickly enough !

Rivers were our nightmares. Whatever people may be led to imagine by motion pictures of Paul Robeson being paddled into a glorious sunset to a rhythm worthy of the Oxford Eight, the average African is *not* river conscious - On the contrary, at the first sight of deep water his senses appear to desert him utterly and he falls into a sort of trance. He offers no co-operation - in fact he is incapable of doing so. He must be pushed or pulled just "so far" but no further. His shoulders must be twisted in just the right direction, till eventually he is sat in the boat, clutching its sides and on his face all the misery of a soapy dog in a bath. It is the only time he does not talk, and the only time too that *all* the Europeans lose all their sense of humour.

Personally I agree with his idea about it. There is no security in a canoe. One is supposed to relax completely but many have proved the fallacy of that theory. Really there is nothing to be done except to hope and concentrate longingly on the other side, while the bilge water, without which no canoe can be found, soaks icily into the seat of your trousers. Actually this and all our other crossings went off with clockwork precision, but I doubt if the average man will ever grow used to them.

With our crossing complete, the stage was now nearly set for the advance of the whole division to begin. The jeep track on the east bank was making rapid progress, the gunners were rapidly closing up, and Divisional Headquarters, housed in bamboo barges, was beginning a stately progress down the river dividing the two Brigades. For two days we lay close to the river bank while the final orders were being planned and issued, and then, early in the morning, our column set off into the hills to the south and east.

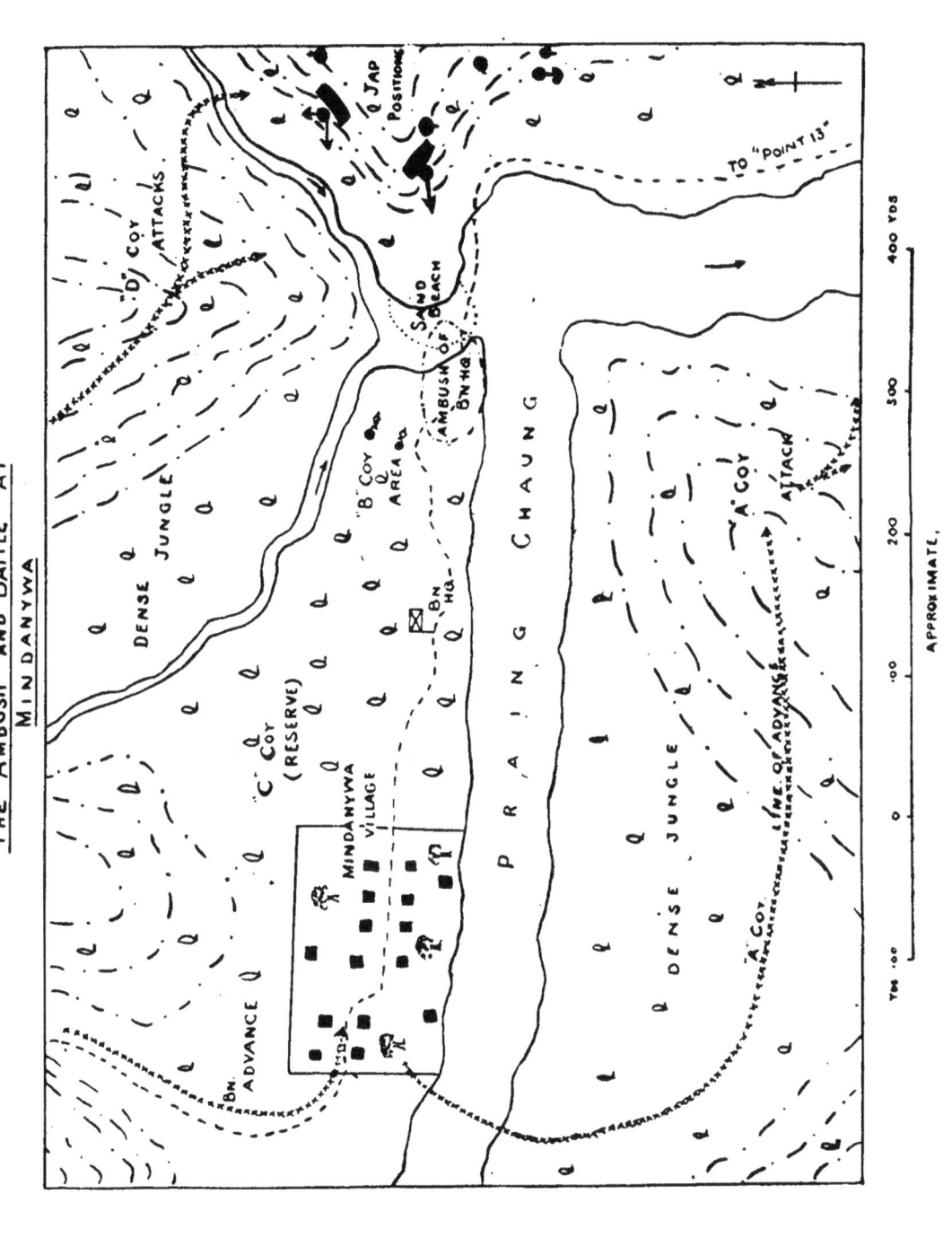

CHAPTER IV

MINDANYWA AND POINT 13

PRIOR to 5th Brigade's move news had been received that the enemy were holding a line from Prugyaung on the Pi Chaung, through Bidonegyaungywa to Kaladan village, and therefore that the direct and obvious route to the south via the Pi Chaung was barred. Prugyaung dominated an area covering the entrance to the 'Soutcol' route, which was known to be important to the Japs, and it was therefore thought that if we demonstrated strongly in that direction, our chances of breaking through somewhere in the centre would be increased.

The Japs had made use of the Soutcol route during their counter offensive early in 1943 when they succeeded in turning our slow advance on Akyab into a very hasty withdrawal. It was one of the few sizeable tracks which joined the valley of the Pi Chaung to that of the Kalapanzin and therefore not lightly to be given up. The same route, it transpired later was to be used again at about this very time, when Col. Tanahashi succeeded in moving a considerable force on to the L. of C. of the 7th Indian Division, and causing much confusion and very fierce fighting for several days.

We ourselves were also to use this route later on in the campaign, but our supplies were to come to us by air whereas the Jap always had to carry every bit of his own.

As at Imphal, one could not help admiring his bold plans; but they were overbold because his conceit led him to underestimate our fighting ability. His second move to Taung Bazaar only served to show his lack of versatility, though that was a trait we had only just begun to recognise, because the propaganda with which we had been continually served always seemed to lay stress his magic qualities in our every efforts to minimize them, with the result that lessons took much longer to learn than they ever should have done. Almost from the original retreat the flood of pamphlets which was released to us had but one theme: "Know your enemy; Learn from the Japs:" "The Jap is *not* a Superman" etc. Anything better designed to create an inferiority complex can hardly be imagined.

In our case the Jap was very easily taken in. With the 1st Gambia threatening Kaladan and the 7 G.C.R. pressing on the Pi Chaung, he thinned out his forces in the centre in the effort to deny these areas, and 8 G.C.R. and then the remainder of 5th Brigade slipped through it with practically no opposition.

We moved rapidly southwards, while the main body of 6th Brigade cleared the east bank of the Kaladan river. It was not easy going. The country still ran north to south in a corrugation of ridges and narrow valleys and we splashed through mud and water for many miles a day. The Brigadier allowed no flagging. "Push on! Push on," was always the cry from behind. Although this meant taking a certain amount of risk in these narrow defiles, I think it was the right policy. We should have spent weeks instead of days in ensuring that those tangled hills were clear.

As the Divisional Commander once put it : "the leading troops *must* be prepared to buy it, if we are to get anywhere". So we hurried along the river beds, sinking deep into the mud, crossing continually from one bank to the other and taking a chance at every corner.

As we made progress scraps of news began to filter in from the villages through which we passed. One or two old men still remained among the silent houses, and they greeted us and told us what they could. The Japanese were not far ahead, they said, and we now knew this must be true for there had been more than one surprise patrol clash as the column went along.

On 16th February we were approaching the village of Mindanywa when our foremost patrol leader came back to report. How much trouble might we have avoided if we had known our jobs better and had more carefully analysed his information! instead of that, being pressed for time, we allowed him to give only an outline of what he knew and then failed to sit down to study all the possibilities which even a map might have made clear to us. The Japs were in the area of the village. Probably they had gone by now. Push on! So 'B' Company was sent ahead to see that the way was clear, while the remainder of the battalion waited impatiently for the signal to go on again.

In an air of supressed excitement now that at last the possibility of a contact was near, we watched the last files of 'B' Company disappear silently round a corner on the track, and seized the chance to call for the inevitable cup of tea. We talked in low voices. Officers fidgeted and checked up on the sentries to see that every approach was covered. Wireless sets were being tested. Then the battery commander stroller in to get the latest news, and stayed on over a cup of tea to retail the latest gossip, which only he ever seemed to have heard. We laughed and joked, but it was rather like the period in which one sharpens pencils before an examination and the minutes dragged by just as on such occasions they are always supposed to drag. As an extra precaution we sent off 'D' Company along the top of the hills to our left so that they might come out in rear of the village, but that was a matter which took but a few minutes to dispose of. The C.O. could not sit down. "Its only a mile," he fretted, after what seemed an interminable time. "What the hell are they playing at?" It was true of course, but a mile along a narrow path in dense jungle can be a very long way.

A Burmese village is never a pleasant place to comb out. Many of them in this area had small but awkward stockades around them, with steps leading over them where the main path enters the village. The method we adopted to deal with them was first to block the various exits, then to cover the main open space by fire, and finally to send in an assault party with grenades ready and LMGs at the hip. We knew what was required, but had never had the time to practise it. It may seem a simple enough operation but it required, good team work, a strong nerve and an eye like a hawk for there are so many little nooks and crannies which a Jap delights to hide in. He can fire straight through the walls of houses, seeing without ever being seen, from dark holes underneath them, from among the wood piles, or from the hencoops. Then there are the tobacco patches; and always the thick, deep green and rather sinister mango-trees -sinister at least until by standing right underneath them you can be quite sure no one is among the branches. Very rightly, its troops not yet having fired a shot, 'B' Company were taking no chances.

After seventy minutes the C.O. could contain himself no longer.

"I'll take on B.H.Q.", he said. "We must find out what's happening. Send the rest along after me when you're ready." He then set off down the track with the "Ack-Ack" Platoon fastening their belts as they hurried to keep up with him. In another ten minutes the remainder of the battalion was in motion and the long column began to wind its way by the tortuous path to the village.

The Jap L.M.G. is of much smaller calibre than the Bren, which gives forth a comforting, friendly roar when it echoes through the bamboo. The former fires very rapidly but its most unpleasant characteristic in the high crackling note of its bullets passing overhead. It is hard to explain why, but it certainly got on the nerves, perhaps in the same way that certain music causes a dog to howl. This particular one gave forth at just the moment that we were creeping through a rocky defile - first just one rapid crackle, and then a veritable tornado of automatic fire, coupled with the very loud explosions of Japanese grenades. Then we heard the much sharper explosions of our "36's" and the roar of Brens. After the silence of a moment before it was a formidable overture to our first battle.

Hearing this so far on the left of our column, I felt certain that "D" Company had come in on the flank, and I hurried forward through the waiting file of riflemen and carriers to the village.

It turned out to be far from the case. 'B' Company commander looked serious coming back to meet me as I watched the troops, looking a little startled, taking cover quietly among the houses. What had happened ? "Well", he explained, "it looks to me as if B.H.Q. and the C.O. have properly bought it." He went on to say that they had just finished clearing the village when B.H.Q. arrived. The C.O. had told him to wait for the battalion while he himself pushed straight through, and - apparently - straight into a strong position half a mile beyond. "Half of them are in a completely open space, pinned down," he said, "and the C.O. is in the middle of it. I've got a platoon down there trying to give them enough covering fire for them to crawl out of it." 'D' Company it appeared had not yet arrived.

We hurried forward together along the track, with our orderlies at our heels. It was not a pleasant situation. Apparently the four leading men had been killed outright; others were wounded, and most of the remainder were lying still and hoping for the best behind small tufts of young elephant grass. We were told this by a panting and excited African who came down the path, a bright red weal neatly parting his hair from front to back. He had managed to wriggle backwards into a chaung and had been sent in to report the situation, which was not one which anyone could like. All the runners, clerks and signallers were either scattered on pinned down in the open: there was a distance of over five hundred yards from the forward position to the village, and behind that the remainder of the battalion was strung out on the narrow path for over a mile. Rather ruefully I remember thinking that on no tactical exercise had one ever been presented with quite so much disorganization at the start. It called for instant action without the means to set it in motion and with our hundreds of headloaders hindering all rapid movement. It was never certain either whether the enemy might not suddenly revert from defence to attack, and such an unarmed mass - new to it all - was an unpleasant responsibility.

It is curious, however, how in battle these things seem to have a way of working out themselves. Even our limited training, apparently, was having its effect, for in a very short while people began to appear of their own accord - first a mortar officer, then the company commanders; now a clerk or two and, best of all, some signallers - and it was possible to restore some order out of what so shortly before seemed likely to develop into chaos.

The area in front was exciting but under control. There were occasional bullets cracking overhead or riccochetting with a screaming whirr off the trees. None of them were very near, and the Jap "knee-mortars" were dropping their missiles with obliging accuracy and singular lack of imagination into a nearby chaung. Hidden behind trees our three bren-gunners were firing accurate bursts into the Jap position for just long enough to allow those lying in the open to wriggle back a few yards nearer to safety.

It was getting too late, though, to mount any attack against such a strong position, but the battalion was being quickly disposed to do so later, and, with evening drawing in fast it seemed that the remainder of the ambushed party would be able to slip away unseen in the failing light.

By nightfall, with little of the normal system of communication on which to rely, I seemed to have walked many miles - visits to the forward guns, a word with the supporting mortars; the company arears to be selected, a visit to the R.A.P., and the gathering together of the scattered elements of battalion headquarters. By 1900 hours all except the killed had been got away and the C.O., walking in as if he had merely come back from a visit from Brigade, cursed roundly about the disorganization which appeared to exist. The ensuing silence, however, was more meaning than wordy protests so after a tot of whisky he grinned wryly and withdrew his remarks. Under the circumstances we had been marvellously lucky to get off so lightly.

It took us three days at Mindanywa before we forced the Japs to withdraw. We could not dislodge them. At this point the Praing Chaung ran east and west past the village, a broad sweep of dry shingle with high banks on either side. Then, at the point where the party were ambushed, it turned due south, and it was at the end of a ridge which overlooked the turn from the east bank that the Japs were dug in, thereby covering the river on both its courses. They had constructed little galleries in the hillside and, apart from a practically sheer slope in front of them, there was a minor chaung with fairly deep water in it guarding their position from the north.

We were new to the job. We had heard so much about speed in warfare, and we attacked too soon here to be able to appreciate the ground. The enemy foiled our attempt to get across the river bed when, later in the campaign, they might have suffered heavily in the attempt, and the attacks by "D" Company on the left were defeated just as much by the ground as by anything else. The men could see nothing, and it was disconcerting for green troops to have grenades showered on them from almost directly overhead. Nevertheless, it appeared that we came within an ace success, for a platoon commander later found his lost hat within a few yards of an enemy post. Hearing no sound there, and seeing nothing, he had been drawn off to the noise of battle further away - a typical instance of jungle warfare, from which many little lessons might be drawn.

During the whole period only one Jap had been seen, and after the battle, in spite of all our accurate mortar fire, only one dead body was found. We picked up a few rounds of ammunition on the position, a few grenades; one or two pieces of equipment. Otherwise, but for their neat foxholes, cunningly concealed in the undergrowth, there was little to show that anyone had been there at all.

Three miles from Mindanywa the track divided, one path continuing the line of the valley, the other swinging east through a break in the hills and then south again by Htittaw and along the edge of the paddy fields stretching five miles east to the Kaladan.

Brigade's plan was that the 8th Gold Coast should secure the junction near Htittaw, after which they were to continue the advance due south, while we ran parallel with them down the edge of the paddy. In order to save time they had passed the 8th round our right flank during the battle, and they had cut their own road through the jungle to their objective. On the left, a company patrol of 7 G.C.R. was given orders to proceed by a wide flank move to Htittaw to ascertain whether the place was held. On paper therefore we were in a very strong position to eliminate any enemy from our path, but the result was a very different matter.

The 8th duly reached the junction, reported it clear and pushed on, leaving a platoon to contact us on arrival. The patrol of the 7th also set off but very quickly lost contact because the wireless, with which it was provided, was simply not powerful enough among the hills and thick woods through which we were passing. (We learnt that the bigger 22-Set was the only safe one for detachments). When our left company, therefore, continuing its advance along the top of the ridge, was greeted at the end of it with a burst of bren fire they naturally assumed for a moment that 7 G.C.R's patrol had gone off its course. The interval in which they tried to verify this was just sufficient for the party of Japs, armed with a British weapon, to consolidate themselves against our attack.

Down on the track, which ran underneath the ridge, all seemed peaceful. The leading company had secured the other side of the narrow valley, and had already taken up its positions. The next company - "C" Company - following the track, had reached a subsidiary chaung running in from the east. A patrol had been across it and contact had been made with a patrol of 8 G.C.R. who reported all quiet. But the next moment a platoon of our own was half wiped out: furious and accurate machine gun fire swept through them as they were crossing the same chaung, and so our second battle began.

It might be said that several people were to blame for this second ambush. Should the 8th have held the area more strongly till we were properly established ? Should their platoon commander have scoured the ground more carefully before he reported it clear ? Or should our platoon, taking nothing on trust, have taken greater precautions in crossing that peaceful-looking chaung ? The answer will get us nowhere. I believe that troops, however well grounded,

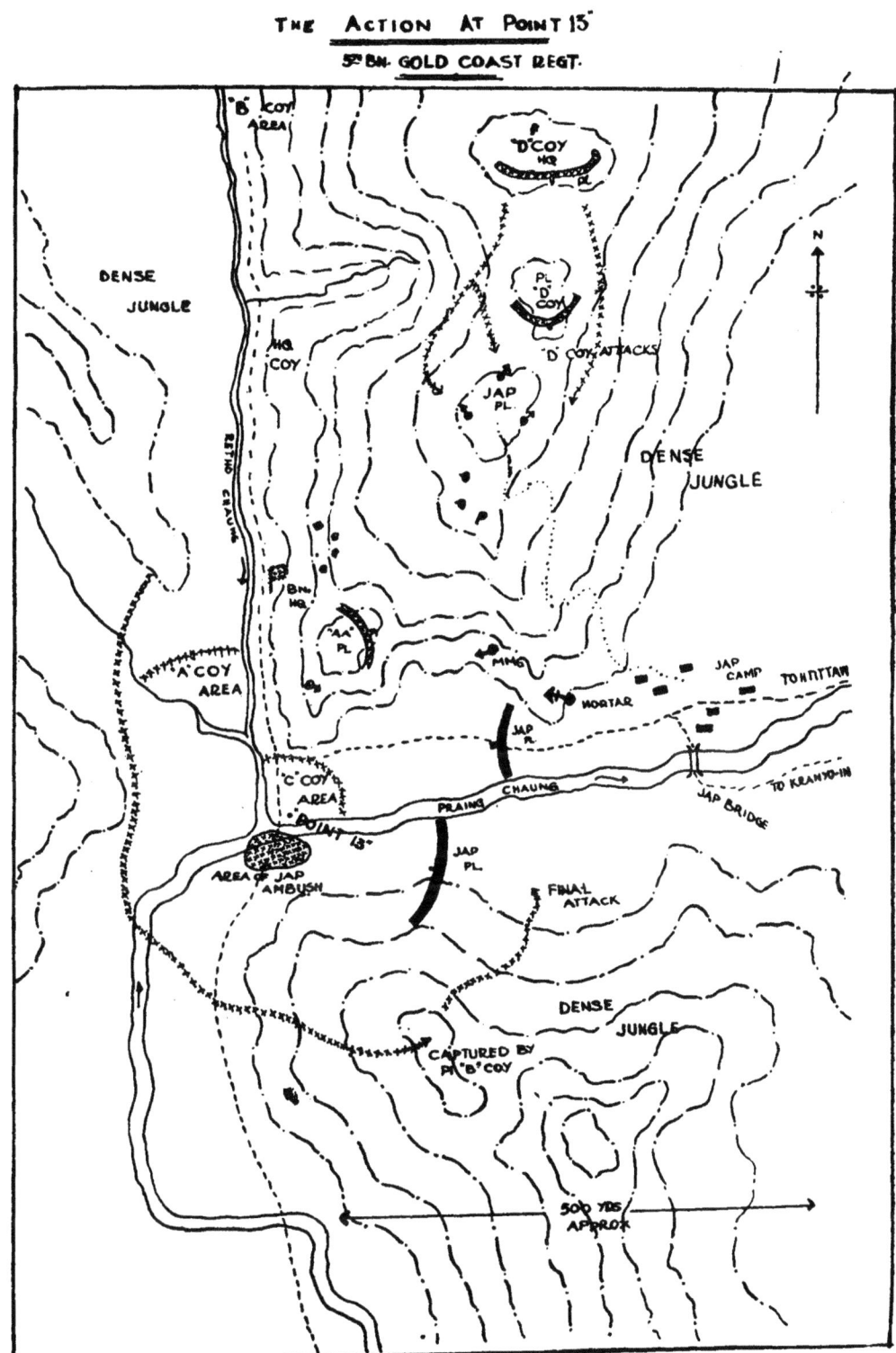

will continue nearly always to make such mistakes when fresh to jungle warfare. Everything is so different. There is no sound: every noise is blanketed by the undergrowth at ten yards, and still more so by the brush and swish of your own movements. A small space stretches innocent before you. Across it it seems hardly credible that you could not detect a position or any movement at so short a range. The overlooking hills, so deep with undergrowth, seem to offer no chance for observation of your progress. There is no field of fire. And so the risk is taken.

We learnt by that second ambush never to trust a yard of ground, however innocent it appeared, and still we were to be similarly surprised on more than one occasion. It is this continual possibility of shattering surprise at point blank range which imposes such a strain on the platoon commander in the jungle - so much so that he maintains that is a real relief when the shooting begins and the fight is on in earnest. The greatest danger is the rather natural fear of being too careful when there are no indications to show that enemy is about.

It took us a further three days to clear the position at Point 13, as this junction was named on the map. There was no sign of the company of 7 G.C.R., who might have taken the position in rear, and the ridge on which 'D' Company was held up became the key position since it overlooked the Japanese flank. The battle for the ridge top surged backwards and forwards in attack and fierce counter attack, but the effect of light automatics and grenades covering a narrow razor-back was too strong for either side. Platoons probed vigorously in many directions, only to find the way barred by machine-gun and mortar fire, but their efforts at least enabled us to use our own mortars with good effect. Then the opposite flank was tried. A round hill to the south of the chaung was cleverly acquired first, and then a groping move through the densest jungle brought a small force onto the enemy's flank. Mortar fire was brought down and during the night the enemy slipped away.

It had been an anxious time for everyone. The position of battalion headquarters, for one thing, close up on the side of the ridge which was so hotly contested, was anything but secure and it was necessary all the time to adjust its rather light defences as the situation shifted in favour of first one side and then the other. In such close contact the night sounds of the jungle played their part in the war of nerves - the rustling of the bamboo-tops and on the jungle floor, the occasional pistol-like crack of cooling bamboo, the hissing and tapping sounds of forest creatures which, till you know them can so easily be interpreted as secret signals; all of these are very disturbing to rest and sleep when the enemy are known to be fifty yards away, and also just above you. Here, too, we were mortared for the first time, and we spent two hours one day attempting to carry on with our duties while listening for that ugly "plop" which hurried us to cover. Some of the bombs fell among the companies, and one or two very near headquarters, but there were no casualties.

In the afternoon the position was captured we spent our time pottering round the dugouts and "bashas" concealed so close behind the Japanese position. One could not help but admire his amazing economy. He has the knack of selecting that *one* post which will conceal him utterly and yet enable him to hold an attack completely. Each gun position is protected by wide-spread and insolated foxholes, dug in the absolute confidence that one man will support the other to the last. There is no spoil to be seen anywhere. Not a branch nor a leaf appears to have been disturbed; yet the field of fire is horribly adequate. His O.P's are seldom discovered, even after all is over, but one may be sure they exist. His mortars are dug into the hillsides, and if his shooting were better he would be a terribly hard nut to crack. Nevertheless he often carries his economy of force too far. There are always places where it is possible to break into his positions, but he risks them, knowing that human nature veers towards the easiest or most obvious approach. To seek the hardest and most unlikely way, with a few well armed and determined men; to infiltrate, widen, and then exploit is probably the most certain way. It is good to take things slowly.

In the peace and quiet after these hard and noisy days it seemed strange to go wandering through this silent Japanese camp. It was so neat in its disorder that it seemed unreal. The houses were beautifully made and cleverly spaced. In them were neat little dolls-house round tables and dolls-house stools raised only a few inches from the ground, but here and there there were dumps of papers, orders, letters and posters in the greatest confusion. We found a set of Japanese postcards, delicate and strangely beautiful in such primitive surroundings, and then smelly places which hurried us on. Spent catridges and pieces of equipment littered the ground, and the I.O., like Walt Disney's Pluto, sniffed widly and joyously around, filling sacks with masses of material for the wretched "I" Staffs further back. Then there was a great temple bell, too heavy for four men to lift, and last of all a scrap of paper scrawled in English in a childish hand.

"Black friends;" it read, "come to us." "Your officers are fools. Very soon Japanese soldier come around your back-side. Look out!"

This was about the final touch to make-belief atmosphere of that funny little camp. Laughingly we added it to our sacks and sent them back. Nobody imagined at the time that it was much more than the childish pastime of some cocky little Japanese private, trying out his English, but in the near future we were to find that the back-side was a very tender part of our anatomy.

CHAPTER V

THE ACTION AT MINTHAZEIK

OUR way from Point 13 led across a beautifully constructed bridge in the little camp, then eastwards along the bank of the chaung through deserted Htittaw, and then south, cautiously along the edge of the yellow paddy fields towards Minthazeik.

"Push on!"

There had been no rest. Almost at once "B" Company had been sent off ahead of us and we soon hurried along in their rear. It was hot and thirsty going now, an anxious work, for we were compelled to cross many wide open areas, overlooked by harmless-looking but none the less menacing hills, which could cover every movement. We must risk them or make little or no progress. The African troops, so long used to the single file of the jungle, took a little time to appreciate this necessity for adopting more open formations in the most dangerous spots.

This enormous rice area we were skirting, so small a part, in actual fact, of the rice producing areas of Burma, gave us some inkling of the importance of this country to the enemy. It stretched for miles - north, east and south - and in the far distance a gold pagoda winked at us from the top of a sharp defined hill, watching our every step. This was the much talked - of Pagoda Hill, standing on the banks of the Kaladan near Kyauktaw, which was considered to be the key to the whole area. We had learnt at Htittaw that the 6th Brigade had captured it, and so felt that it regarded us now with a friendly eye. In a few more days we were to view it in a very different light.

The plain was blazing hot; it actually burnt the feet as we stumbled along over the rough paddy in a cloud of dust. There was little or no water about except in the unpleasant and muddy tanks near the numerous villages we passed. Everywhere else the water holes were depressions of caked and cracking mud, but one could pick out the trace of the dried water courses easily enough by the thin lines of stunted and almost leafless trees which ran haphazard across the plain. Here and there great clouds of grey-blue smoke rose high into the air where the villagers were burning the rice stubble, and vultures swooped and soared above them.

None of the villagers appeared to have left the area. In fact we found that they were crowded with refugees from both north and south. They seemed friendly and quite unperturbed, and crowded on the verandahs or under the mango trees as we wound our way through. At a halt they gave us eggs and evil looking green cheroots in exchange for cigarettes, and told us that the Japs had passed through the night before bearing forty to fifty wounded and several dead. It was good news to us, for the troops had begun to feel a little depressed at finding no visible proof of their progress, just as the Japs had clearly meant them to be.

Late in the afternoon we harboured in a dusty and shadeless area to the sound of sporadic firing away to the south. The advanced guard had reached Minthazeik only to find the river crossing held. But there was no point in pushing on further, for we had marched fifteen miles and were tired out in the unaccustomed heat of the plain. The advanced guard were safely consolidated and the best and easiest thing to do was to get some sleep.

Next morning the C.O. came back after a visit long before breakfast to the forward company. Apparently the chaung which ran across their front was tidal and not fordable, and the Japs were covering the crossing with both light and medium machine guns. There was little hope of forcing it there, with the deep mud and banks vertical and ten feet high. On the other hand the Sierra Leone Regiment had crossed the chaung two or three miles further down, and the obvious move seemed to be for us to make a flank attack from that direction while keeping the Japs fully occupied in front. The C.O. assigned me with two companies to do the job, and gave orders that the attack was to go in next day.

The flat expanse of paddy which stretched across to 'Sierra Leone's' area was not at all a simple matter to cross, and it seemed an interminable time before our small advance party reached the river again. It was not so much the strict orders regarding concealment which slowed down our movement, but the innumerable little chaungs and water courses which had to be negotiated. Every one was tidal, and if the tide was out it was equally an obstacle because the mud must have been the softest and deepest that ever existed. Tanks would have been little value in this country. So we were forced to make long detours to find the few existing footbridges, which themselves were a feat to negotiate. If there were boy-scouts in Burma, one felt, then they must have constructed these. Picking our way over the parched ground between one obstacle and another, one glared up in envy at the Hurricanes roaring overhead and swooping down on distant villages with their cannon barking. No hot sunlight, dust or burning paddy fields for them! However we reached our destination at last, there to find "Sa. L." bathing in the river and preparing to make merry with several cows which the R.A.F. had conveniently bumped off just before their arrival.

It was quite a picnic scene.

"Where are the Japs now?", we asked, as we sat down to their meal.
The Japs? Someone munching hard waved with a fork to an area a few hundred yards away.
"Somewhere over there." About those trees, he thought,
"We're in reserve, though. So why not a picnic?"

We re-crossed the river and set up our HQ in a little dugout on the near side. These were to be found in every village and we had imagined at first that the Japs had made them. It made one feel very sorry for the patient Burmese, the victims of bombing and straffing from either side, forced again and again to work and carry for the Jap, their cattle killed or taken away without payment. We learnt that quite a number of the villagers had been killed by our own aircraft, yet they remained cheerful and friendly, and with few exceptions were prepared to help us all they could. I admired their gentleness and their placid acceptance of hardship.

Soon after dusk the companies loomed up silently in the darkness and the crossing began. There was a powerful current running out and the banks were as slippery as ice, but in spite of their amazing awkwardness in the face of deep water, the men were soon safely across and asleep on the other side.

Our plan for the next day could only be a simple one. There were but two covered approaches to our objective; the one, a belt of scrub and small trees running westwards along the river bank; the other, a dry chaung bed parallel to the river and two or three hundred yards south of it. The second was chosen because, though we should eventually have to leave it and cross an area of open paddy, we should at least have the power to manoeuvre, if necessary, in either direction, north or south. Also because it increased our chances of getting right behind the Jap defences. Once across the paddy we were to move in a series of short bounds to a pimple which we called Hill 50 directly in rear of the enemy's defences. "D" Company were to set off in front and "A" Company were to pass through them when the first bound was reached.

Next morning "Sa. L." were still holding the wide perimeter of the village when the leading troops marched out, yet we had hardly gone more than five hundred yards when a crackle of Jap rifle fire broke out quite close to us on our left flank. It turned out to be a small Jap patrol, but how they had managed to get there - and on green bicycles - we could not imagine! "A" Company quickly drove them off, and our thin column went forward again in the doubtful cover of the chaung bed. Later came the moment for "D" Company to leave it and cross the remaining five hundred yards of open ground to the woods; and it was an anxious moment, for we had long had to abandon all training in methods of open warfare. It was still worse then when we heard the Japs open up from right and left ahead with still four hundred yards to go. But there was no faltering. Extended wide across the open fields, the troops just went on at the same steady pace and the enemy apparently fled into the woods.

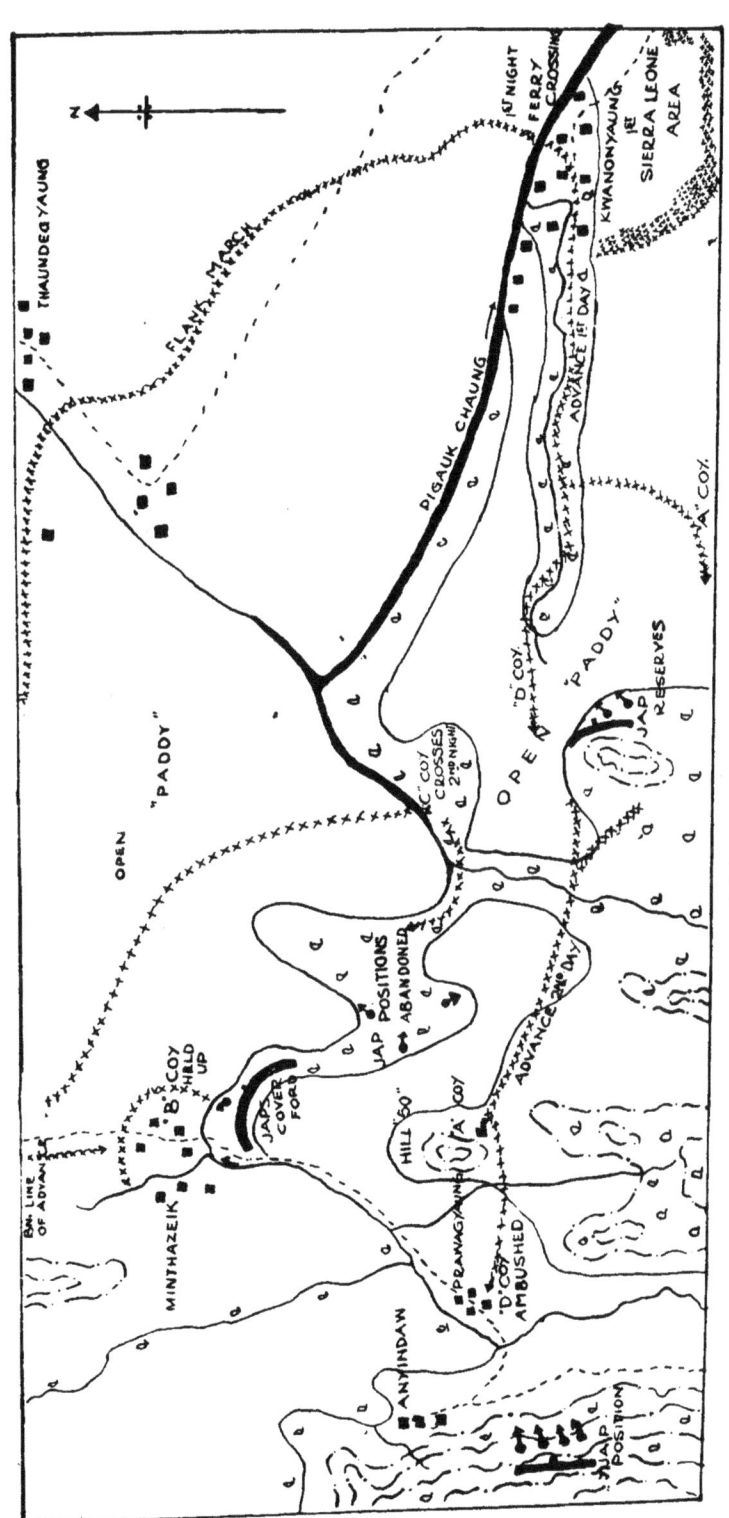

In the meantime "A" Company moved out wide to the left flank and in every short time the whole force reached cover again, there to re-organize for our further advance.

It was now that the real battle began. The woods here were a tangled mass of thorn and undergrowth and, even without opposition, it would only have been possible to advance at a snail's pace. Intercommunication was hopeless, and we became a clumsy force, groping forward in the attempt to remain co-ordinated. The Japs, with no fixed objective, danced round us like terriers and we were attacked from all directions except the rear. In nearly seven hours we managed to advance little more than five hundred yards, and the sultry air vibrated with the thump of grenades, with roaring brens and the rapid crackle of the Jap L.M.Gs. We should have made better progress if our section commanders had been more experienced, but it might not have been a great deal better. Unless a fairly rigid formation was maintained it would have been as easy to have fired on friend as on foe.

Curiously enough, it was the Japs who suffered the casualties. For all their speed and determination in counter attack, they could make no headway against our automatics, and even less in face of our grenades. In one case at least nine of them were killed in vain attempts to bring in three of their wounded, and the shreiks and screams in other areas - although nothing could be seen - proved that our weapons were taking deadly effect. The troops were firing their grenades from discharger cups, with the rifle held almost parallel to the ground. It was a method we often used. The fierceness of the engagement is illustrated by the fact that three times during the day different platoons were reported as being surrounded. If the Japs had the initiative, however, the battle continued to move in our favour.

Quite early in the proceedings the rice stubble was set on fire by tracer bullets, and the crackle of the flames filled in the short periods of silence. The drifting smoke increased our already raging thirst. Then in the afternoon, just when slight progress was evident, the wind took a hand and the flames flared up and spread rapidly towards us. In the short space of an hour our headquarters had to be shifted three times, with the fire driving us first one way and then, cussedly back again. The foremost platoon sent in a runner to say that they might not be able to hang on to the position they had reached on account of it, while the Japs on the other hand seized the advantage and took the opportunity to shoot us up from several unexpected directions. The whole day was a confusion of sound and smoke and unexpected movement.

Late in the afternoon, however, the firing slowly died away and the companies pushed forward to their next objective, where it was decided to consolidate. The men were exhausted, the ammunition was running short, and there was no water. We were just reporting this over the R/T, however, when the two grinning quartermasters appeared - well ahead of time - with gallons of hot tea and huge 'chatties' of water scrounged from the nearby villages. They had come calmly through the area with about forty to fifty men and perhaps six rifles between the lot of them.

The troops looked tired but very pleased with themselves as they set about digging their new positions in the falling light, while they carefully cleaned their weapons and recounted lucky escapes. One of them pointed out a tree which had been cut into by an enemy L.G.M. as if someone had applied an axe to it, and the gunner who had been behind it jumped grinning to his feet to show that he was still very much alive. Someone else produced a hat with a neat hole through the crown and another, a battle dress blouse, which had been shot to ribbons across the chest without touching the man's skin. I have never ceased to marvel at the escapes one heard of - a buckle hit, a watch smashed, clothing riddled: on one occasion a roll of papers withstood a direct hit on an officer's thigh. The most extraordinary, perhaps, was the case of a man who was hit on the cheek by a grenade which then exploded at his feet, and the scratch on his face was all he had to show for it. The Japanese hand grenade is very noisy, but that is about all.

During the night there was no disturbance, and "C" Company managed an unopposed landing across the river into the wood away on our right. The advance continued again early next morning, and we then went forward unopposed to our objective, finding abandoned machine gun positions, cunningly concealed, which might have caused us a good deal of trouble. "A" Company secured Hill 50 and then "D" passed through it to the village of Prawagyaumg which lay a few hundred yards further west. "C" Company, combing the woods along the Praing Chaung, was making for the main river crossing to cover the battalion across.

It was now approaching midday and not a shot had been fired, and we were just settling down in the believe that all was over when hell broke loose in the direction of the hills to the west. It was another sad example of an excellently planned Jap ambush. Knowing that we should have to secure the track leading south from the river crossing, they had occupied concealed positions on the ridge overlooking it. They had allowed a part of D company to pass through the village, and then brought down everything they had on Company Headquarters and the unarmed carrier groups.

For ten minutes there was a tornado of rifle and machine-gun fire, of bursting grenades and mortars and the sharp detonations of a quick-firing anti-tank gun. Then complete silence. It was the way things always were happening.

Though the casualties were actually surprisingly light, the battalion suffered a severe loss in the deaths of C.S.M. O'Shea and the company commander, Capain Painter, in this ambush. Painter had been a magnificent leader. During the last three weeks his company had managed to get involved in all the fighting. He himself was always in the most important place. He never interfered with platoons, but in the hottest moments always seemed to be able to make his presence felt. A gallant failure was never enough for him. He probed tried again and again, and worried on until the Jap had enough. He knew every man, and the troops loved him. They were so depressed by his loss that it required strenuous efforts to shake them out of their resulting apathy, a state which the African is inclined to on occasions because he seems to have no sense of revenge which might help to offset his other feelings.

The stage was now set for the Brigade's advance southwards to Apaukwa. The action had been quite a hot one, but it clearly demonstrated that the Japs are not prepared to hold a position once their rear is threatened, or when they are compelled to fight outside their carefully prepared defences. It demonstrated very clearly to us the absolute necessity of something better than communication by runner in very dense jungle. The junior commander can exercise little tactical influence once close contact has been made, but at least in normal warfare he is able to do so in advance by means of the plan he makes of and of the clarity of the orders he issues. But in the jungle - because he can see nothing - it is often impossible to make a co-ordinated plan, and it is therefore much more important as the battle progresses that he should be quickly informed as to the progress being made and the nature of the ground encountered. The runner could never do this, and the "walkie-talkie"- which we could not get - was the only answer.

We were given a day's rest after Minthazeik, and then once again our patrols were pushed forward preparatory to the next move south. The move, in fact, had actually begun, and we were groping forward by night, when an order arrived suddenly for our withdrawal. For over a fortnight we had been living in a world of our own, and the rapid change in the situation on 6th Brigade's front was quite unknown to us. It was therefore rather a shock to us to receive that order. So far as we knew, everything had been going well. Kyauktaw had been found clear of the enemy. Pagoda Hill had been taken with hardly a struggle. Thereupon the direction of 6th Brigade's thrust had been switched and the greater part of them were operating on our left, on the same side of the river as we and a good deal further south.

In the early hours of the morning we got back to the battalion harbour, and the next day we began to retrace the dusty way we had come, rather bewildered and still quite unaware of the troubles in store for us.

CHAPTER VI

"COX'S CORNER"

As a whole the 81st Division had reached its furthest point south at Kyauktaw, although the Nigerians had pushed on as far as Apaukwa. It had been intended to turn westwards at this point to strike the Japanese right flank near Htizwe, on the main Arakan front, but the plan had had to be abandoned. In the first place the amphibious operations near Akyab had suddenly to be called off for reasons connected with the European front, and then revised orders were issued which were not really possible to carry out. The Division was then only to demonstrate towards the Arakan, but at the same time the Pagoda Hill area was to be regarded as vital.

As events turned out it became essential to concentrate our whole force in the latter area, because it was the Japs who seized the initiative at this moment, striking swiftly in considerable force. Therefore the order did not greatly signify. But it showed a misconception of the make-up and weakness of our formation which may also exist still in the mind of the reader.

The 81st Division was a special force, quite unlike any normal Indian division. In the Kyauktaw area it actually had some M.T., but this consisted of no more than a few jeeps and 30-cwts, mainly for the use of the 3.7 Howitzer batteries and divisional signals. There were no mules. Every other piece of equipment, and all supplies, were carried on the men's heads. Taking an average load at 45 lbs., it can be seen that the number of headloaders for even the minimum amount of equipment must be very considerable, nearly equalling the number of fighting men. The vast majority of these headloaders were unarmed except for the matchet, which every African carries. Supplied as we were by air, there could be no front nor L. of C., and so it was very important that this huge, helpless body should be adequately protected at all times. And it was this that was our main difficulty, since the 3rd Brigade had been taken away for a special task before the campaign began.

There were two main courses of action which could have been taken on receipt of the order. The first was to divide the force in half, using only one Brigade for the diversionary role; the second was to hold the Pagoda Hill area very lightly and to push the bulk of the force towards Htizwe. But there were objections to *both* courses, because the orders implied *two* main tasks. The whole purpose of the Kaladan campaign was to assist the offensive on the main Arakan front, yet the order stated that the Kyauktaw area must be held without fail, implying an exact division of responsibility when only two brigades were available. To send but one brigade on the diversionary role would have been a most hazardous operation with such inexperienced and ill-supported troops, yet to send more would have laid open the Kyauktaw area, which was by no means suitable for defence. The decision was made for the diversionary role, which was why the bulk of 6th Brigade were on the west bank of the river when the Japanese counter-stroke was delivered.

It may be that the Kyauktaw area was held more lightly than it should have been. On the night of March 1st 1944 the East African Scouts - a purely reconnaissance unit - under-armed, and hastily organized in 1943, were violently attacked at Thayettebin, north east of Pagoda Hill. They had neither artillery nor mortar support, and after bravely withstanding two massed attacks during the night, they were broken and scattered at dawn by the third. In the mean time the 1st Gambia Regiment had very hurriedly been given the task of defending Pagoda Hill, and a move was at once made to withdraw the 4th Nigerians and 1st Sierra Leone, who were already well to the south.

The "Gambias" failed to hold their position. Their dispositions apparently were hastily selected, the enemy infiltrated between them and, in spite of heavy casualties, finally overran the position and seized Pagoda Hill. It now became evident that it was too late to retrieve the situation by pushing reinforcements across the Kaladan, so it was decided to make a rapid withdrawal northwards whence it would be feasible to strike east to counter any further move by the enemy. It was also obvious that with Pagoda Hill held by the Japs the whole area west of it, with its scanty cover, was quite untenable.

It was this state of affairs, of which we were sublimely ignorant, which was the reason for the rapid about-turn of our own battalion after Minthazeik.

We had all read the text books on the moral effect of a withdrawal, but none of us had any idea how true the teaching was. It had seemed even less likely to be so in our case, supplied as we were by air. Why in these circumstances we had argued, should a move in one direction effect us any more than a move in the other? In this case, too, we were informed of the reason for our withdrawal, and it seemed to us fair enough and above board. There seemed no reason to be down-hearted about it. But we were in a great hurry. It would be all right, we told ourselves, if the troops were told about it a little later. What a mistake we made!

How few are the operations which succeed quite in going according to plan. In our case, when the withdrawal began, our particular task was to adopt a flanking position towards Pagoda Hill to cover the movement of the remainder of the Brigade. We were to have held that for at least twenty four hours and then - in an orderly manner - to close up to them on the next bound. In actual fact nothing of the kind occurred. We were moved and counter-moved; the tempo became quicker and quicker, and in the end we were quite unable to tell the troops the situation because we were just as perplexed as they were.

It will not be easy to forget the picture of the Division's withdrawal, though the details may quickly fade - how the atmosphere rapidly changed from a feeling of order and confidence to one of vague depression and exasperation. The golden pagoda, gleaming in the sunshine from the far bank of the Kaladan, suddenly ceased to look benevolent and calmly beautiful, but became instead a place of evil, from which cunning Japanese eyes might follow every movement and direct his artillery fire accurately amongst us. The great flat rice plain seemed to grow ever hotter, the dust ever denser and more irritating, and the existing cover still less adequate than we had imagined it before.

The first day was exhausting, spent in the hot sun reconnoitring an exposed position in a dirty and burnt out village in the middle of the plain. There was much to do. There was the best line of approach to be decided; a bridge to be found rather better than the normal boy-scout contraptions which our carriers would hardly be able to negotiate; a forming-up place which could provide cover for the hundreds of men waiting to occupy their new areas, and canoes to be hunted out of their places of concealment so that communication could be possible among that multitude of chaungs. There was also the burdensome responsibility of selecting tactically sound positions in the open for a battalion which had never trained in the open for over a year. Then, late in the afternoon, when the task was done and the troops were about to move into their new positions, another order came through and we were turned reluctantly back to the area we had only abandoned that morning.

In the previous night "B" Company had been suddenly hustled off northwards to secure a crossing over the Pi Chaung, from which the thrust eastwards to re-establish contact with the Jap was to begin. On this night "A" Company followed it, and the remainder of the battalion was ordered to act as rear-guard to the brigade. And so the next day we began the slow tramp northwards at the tail of a huge column, cursing the jeeps and other vehicles which edged by, choking us with their dust, and envying the Hurricanes which looked so cool and clean up in the sky. Away to the right another long column moved across the paddy in a drifting screen of dust and further to the north-east high dust pillars indicated the movement of vehicles, all converging on the one bridge which could carry them most quickly northwards. The evil gold pagoda seemed now to be moving along with us, but the whole day not a shell was fired.

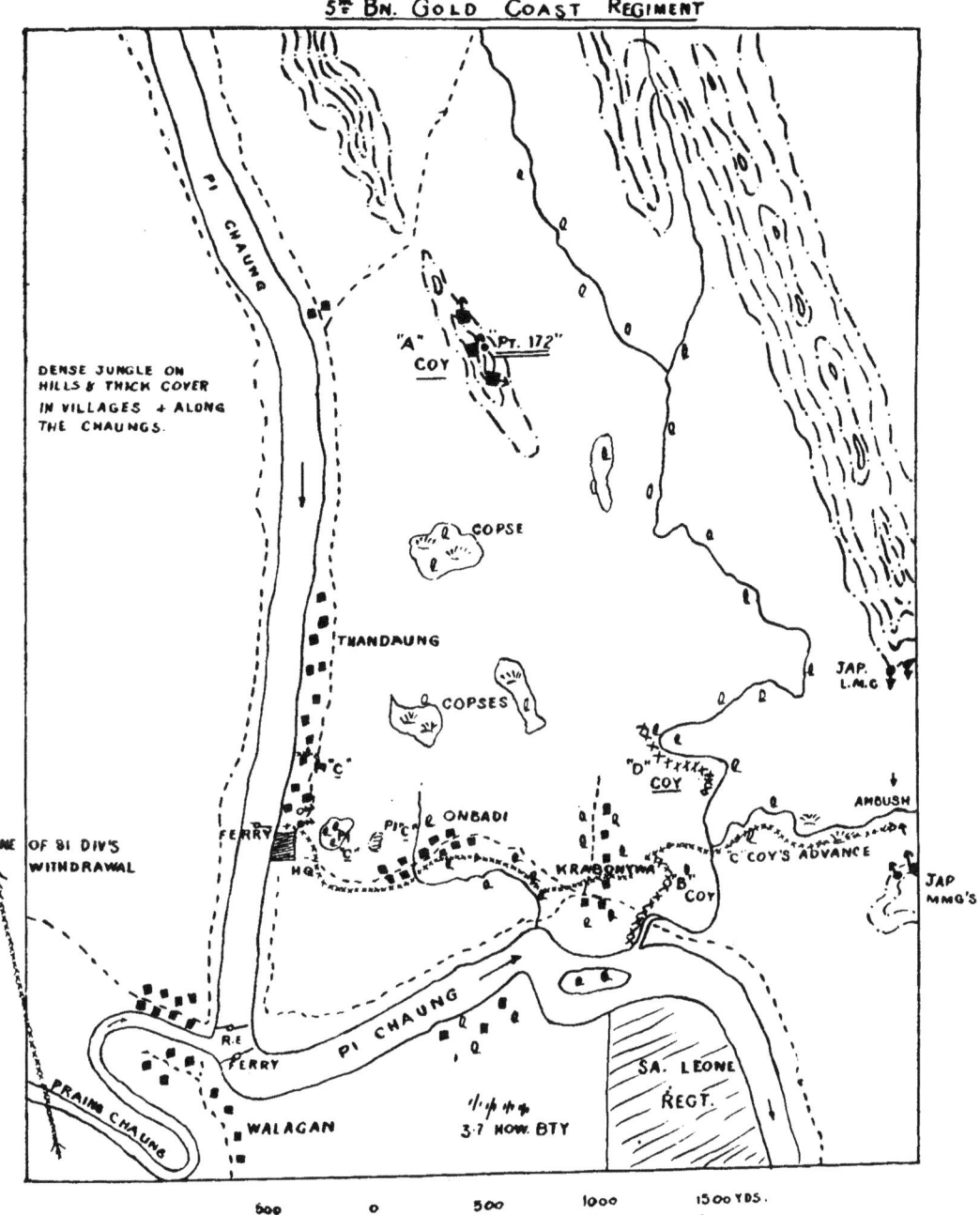

The mile long village of Walagan, when at last we got there, seemed a place of chaos, though nobody else seemed to notice it. Different columns double-banked under the coconut trees, jeeps and trailers edged between them, and the engineers, staggering with their folding boats on top of eight men's heads, cheerfully held up the lot. It seemed impossible that order could ever be achieved, yet within the hour there was room for everybody to move and by dusk our river crossing was well under way.

The area of the new bridgehead was known as "Iraq". It did not look too healthy. At this point the Pi Chaung, three hundred yards wide, forms a right angle bend as it runs down from the north and then turns sharply east towards the Kaladan. For nearly a thousand yards along each of its arms, and in the space between, the ground is mainly flat but broken up by patches of dense cover and by two elongated villages which formed a letter "T". The whole area is overlooked by high ground to the north and east and the two main approaches to it are separated by a distance of over a mile. It was this area which 5 G.C.R. was to be prepared to hold, in order first to protect the concentration of the brigade and then to enable it to cross.

Tactically it would have been soundest if we had pushed well forward into the hills, but there was no indication when the brigade would be ready to cross and in order to cover all the likely approaches further forward we should have been compelled to spread ourselves over a wide area in 'penny packets'. In this particular instance, also, the issue was further complicated by the fact that "Brigade" had ordered us to hold the line of a subsidiary chaung about eight hundred yards east of the crossing place. Such an order was wrong in principle and it was also a misjudgment for, far from providing a suitable obstacle, the chaung afforded covered approaches from several directions without any compensating fields of fire. An alteration might have been insisted upon, but as it was the remaining companies had to be disposed to conform with it. Thus there were three companies placed forward in a wide arc, with but one in depth, while battalion headquarters took up position in the centre with a mass of unarmed soldiers of the Field Ambulance and Auxiliary Group in a narrow wood along the banks of the Pi Chaung.

When we took up these positions at Iraq there was little indication that 5 G.C.R. was about to endure the most dangerous and the hardest battle of both the campaigns they fought. Not a single shot had been fired during the hot and tiring rush back from Minthazeik, and neither "A" nor "B" Companies were molested during the hours they held the area before our arrival. That night, however, a patrol of 8 G.C.R. had bumped a Japanese position a mile or two in front of "B" Company and evidently scared them badly, for we lay awake under the stars listening to them blazing away for over two hours. There was no reply from our own weapons for the simple reason that the patrol had immediately faded away into the darkness. A platoon of our own, sent forward to secure the high ground well in front, met nothing.

Next morning it was decided to send "C" Company forward further to secure the hills, to the east, and when they had done so the battalion was due to follow. Under the trees in the morning sunlight we sat peacefully eating our breakfast, waiting patiently and without excitement for their progress reports to come in. No shooting could be heard anywhere, in fact hardly a sound could be heard save for the peaceful drone of reconnaissance aircraft and the muffled stutter of river-craft, down by the ferry.

Suddenly at about ten o'clock a tremendous wave of firing broke and continued for a considerable time. We could easily distinguish the Jap machine gun fire, both medium and light, and the bursts of our own grenades and mortars, but there was no reason to assume that there was anything wrong because by this stage of the campaign we had grown used to these startling changes from peace to pandemonium. Once the Jap *does* open up he is not mean; he lets off whole magazines in one burst and the African gives him measure for measure. It was therefore very much of a shock when suddenly a number of dazed-looking Africans appeared out of the woods in front of us, quite obviously very disorganized.

They were brought in to battalion headquarters and we questioned them there anxiously, though it was difficult to get much sense out of them. The more coherent said that they seemed to have been opened up on from all sides: their company HQ had been cut off from the start, the ammunition had run out and then the enemy had charged in firing machine guns from the hip. This was all the information we could get for a long time, and no more men came back. Most of those who had were from the ammunition echelon and were unarmed. For the moment the wireless was dead. It appeared later that many of the Europeans had been forced to hide under bushes or sham dead among the victorious Japs. The firing continued but it began to die down slowly.

Some time later a British sergeant came in - an ex-commando - exhausted, dazed and covered with mud. Much of what we had already learnt was true, apparently. He told us that at one moment he had been set upon by six Japs, three of whom he had bayoneted, and he had then been forced to crawl through a muddy chaung bed to avoid the others all around. The company commander, he was sure, had been killed; probably the second-in-command also. The trouble had been that the forward troops were cut off from their ammunition reserves.

Still later two very junior subalterns came back with their platoons, and last of all a platoon sergeant, who had lain for hours under a bush hoping to get away the body of his company commander. It had been a highly successful ambush - from the Jap point of view.

Of course it was now obvious from all the various reports that the enemy's numbers in front of us were quite considerable - probably at least a battalion and possibly more - and it made it a fairly serious situation. "C" Company was certainly badly shaken by the ambush; yet they were our only reserve, while the very wide front we were holding would have made a break-through difficult to hold at any time. As one can see from the sketch, there was a very wide gap between "D" Company and the right of "A" who were on point 172, and it should have been an easy enough matter for the Japs to have infiltrated between them to strike either of these two companies in rear. If their forces happened to be strong enough to hold one of them while attacking the other, there seemed little prospect of our being able to sort out the mess.

We sent a message to Brigade asking for reinforcements, which came eventually and remained with us to a short while, but, at the moment, they said there were no boats available, and we were told that it would be at least two hours before they could begin crossing. Thus with three companies widely spread out and by no means in the best positions we were left waiting, not very hopefully, for the next Japanese move.

The reason for "C" Company's ambush was inexperience and lack of training, and nothing else. It might, and usually does happen to a part or whole of any unit newly embarked on its first campaign. Into the little chaung along which "D" Company was posted, there ran a dry and shallow water course, with its source, quite near the foot of the hills, which was the objective. Close on either side of it the ground was flat and open, and beyond it the hills rose up in an arc, running from the left to straight in front of them. Further to the right there was a smallish knoll, standing in the centre of the open fields. On this knoll, and at the base of the hills all round, the Japs had concealed themselves so that their guns and mortars could cover the water course from both sides. And it was this water course that the company had chosen as its line of advance.

It would have been an elementary precaution, of course, to have sent forward a strong fighting patrol, first to test the ground in front and to secure an area the other side, but as it happened nothing like that was done. The whole company set off as one. The mortars also moved with the company - much too far forward - with the result that when the firing broke out they were unable to give support until they had moved back a considerable distance. There were no L.M.Gs. placed on the ground to cover the flanks of such a vulnerable target, and so the Japs were enabled to break in and disorganize the column completely. The officers had neither the drill nor battle sense to anticipate such obvious possibilities.

Nevertheless, though none of us realized it at the time, the affair had been by no means the walk-over that one might imagine. Although the company commander and his 2 i/c were killed almost at once, the men managed to inflict a considerable number of casualties on the enemy and the mortars later put in some very sterling work. The main reason why they had eventually to abandon their position was because the ammunition echelon had been cut off by a wide area of fire-swept ground and so were unable to get forward to the fighting troops. The mortar men had had to cross this area before taking up their firing positions, and one or two of the Africans had shown great bravery in re-crossing it to retrieve vital equipment from some of their wounded comrades. The casualties inflicted just gave us sufficient time to re-organize for the inevitable follow-up which came in later.

When the second attack began the enemy let slip a golden opportunity. If they had done the right thing, they would in all probability have driven us out of the bridgehead, for the troops were jittery and their ammunition would undoubtedly have run out. The sketch shows the large gap existing between "A" and "D" Companies, but it does not show the useful patches of cover which were strewn about it, which would have enabled the enemy to have infiltrated slowly wherever they pleased. It was demonstrated instead that the Jap - whose good points had only been written about - was neither above making grave mistakes nor failing completely to appreciate a situation.

Back in battalion headquarters we heard the furious firing break out again, and it was an exciting hour. All the time we were expecting to catch a glimpse of the little brown-clad figures, creeping forward to the edge of the village in front of us and opening up with their crackling automatics into the middle of our crowded wood. "C" Company would not be much value - several of them were still coming in - and there were only two L.M.Gs. of the "Ack-Ack" platoon besides. But none appeared. For some time the heavy firing still went on and then slowly began to die away. When the little battle at last died down the company commander supplied the answer. The enemy apparently had misjudged the size of the objective. In massed formation they had charged "D" Company in the centre, where they had ran into a murderous fire from the left platoon. They had persisted for a bit - as they always will - but then our artillery had been brought down amongst them and they broke and fled.

It was just as well. One of the platoons had run completely out of ammunition and the other two were so short that they could only have gone on for another fifteen minutes.

It was about that time we were given an interesting sidelight on the procedure at a forward Japanese HQ. A man in "C" Company, who had been captured that morning, had just come in. Apparently he had been brought before the Jap commander who, after a perfunctory question or two, had shrugged his shoulders arrogantly and ordered the man to sit down while he continued the battle. During the attack on "D" Company, the African said, this officer remained seated all the time on a tiny chair. Every two or three minutes runners came running in from every direction to give their information. Hardly stopping as they came through, they shouted their messages at the top of their voices; the officer shouted back at them, and then they went trotting on again to their units. Nobody had thought it worth while to pay any attention to the simple African, so in the middle of a shouting match he quietly faded out and made his way back to the unit. Of the few of our troops who were captured, most of the others managed to do a fade-out in the same manner.

It had been agreed by now that, in view of the enemy strength, there was no question of sticking to the plan of gaining the hills in front of us. If the Japs had got there first it would be a matter of days to drive them out, and the situation elsewhere - to say nothing of the sector which we held - washed out any possibility of bigger forces being drafted into the area. Later in the afternoon we learnt that the divisional plan had been changed. It was too late now to mount the attack eastwards, and a further and rather tricky withdrawal was to be made to the north. Our role was to act as flank guard, so we were told to remain and hold on to what we had got.

As the afternoon wore on without further action but with all the constant activity in a battalion headquarters, it became clear to us that there was a strong possibility we might be in an unenviable position before we were due to leave. We ourselves were confined in an area unsuitable for defence, while at the same time the division had to pass through a bottleneck formed by the only bridge available. If the Japs had any sense they could exploit the situation to the full: they could attempt to drive us into the river in order to harass the bridge by small arms fire; they could cause a great deal of chaos everywhere by even minor concentrations of artillery, and they could press so hard from the south that certain elements - i.e. ourselves - might almost certainly have to be left behind in order to ensure the remainder getting clear. It was inevitable that such considerations should occur to us, even if in rather a vague and cloudy manner, and they served to heighten the tension as the time went on.

Towards dusk the battle broke out again. Until it is over, you can never tell what is happening on such occasions. A company commander is far too busy in a close range infantry fight to be able to send messages about it. So we had to sit about once again with one ear glued to the telephone, listening to the crack of rifle fire, the furious bursts - much too long - of the Brens, to the loud bursts of Jap grenades and the curious muffled and concentrated explosions of our own. It was impossible to tell how things were going, but at long last we heard the welcome sound of our own artillery to the south of the Pi Chaung and quite soon afterwards the firing died away with the few parting rifle shots which end every action.

The telephones tinkled and you could almost feel the drop in tension. The first words were an urgent demand for more ammunition. Then the story came through. The attack had been strongly pressed in fairly large numbers, but once again the Japs had failed to find the gap. This time, attacking "B" Company, they had once more been caught in enfilade by a flank platoon and had had the guns brought down in the middle of them as they wavered.

The company commander seemed pretty pleased. "There's an awful stink here," he said cheerfully. "The blighters are running like hell. They've set the bush alight and they're chucking their dead bodies into it as they go by."

For the moment we could relax. It was good news. We sat watching some stretcher cases and one or two walking wounded moved slowly towards us across the paddy; and half listened to the I. O. passing on the news to the other companies and back to Brigade. With the approaching darkness nothing much could be done. Nearby the R.S.M. stood checking ammunition and preparing to send a party off. He looked rather anxious but said nothing. There was nothing much he could say. Two months later he told me that he was left then with but one 1000-round box of S.A.A. in reserve, and that no more supplies arrived from Brigade for a further eight hours.

However to our surprise and relief nothing happened during the night. Quite possibly the enemy hoped we should conform to the rules by counter-attacking them. But we were much too tired and unsure of ourselves for that. Well after dawn there were no signs of any activity and we were able to eat our breakfasts in peace.

The order now came through that we should be withdrawn after nightfall - if all went well - which was a good deal sooner than we had expected. Very mistakenly the news was passed on, and in an hour or so every man knew about it. The effect was immediately noticeable. Hitherto they had been resigned to an indefinite period in Iraq but now, like schoolboys at end of term, I think we all began unconsciously to count off the hours till the strain would be ended, with this unpleasantly broad river in front of us instead of at our backs. People began to wonder if the boats would arrive on time; if they would turn up at all; and especially if the Jap, who always seemed to take action at the most uncomfortable times, would discover our intentions, with all the implications that gave rise to. If we had not been hard on the go for over a fortnight it might have made no difference, but in the circumstances it strained the unarmed soldiers to nearly breaking point and made the hours for all of us seem like enternity.

The quiet continued all through the morning, but most of us, I think, would have preferred something to happen. This was the first time that we had had to deal with Japanese snipers, and quite the worst time too. Nobody had believed that they could not be found, as the pamphlets implied, but at any rate all our efforts to do so came to nothing here. The villagers, too, were particularly suspect: whether it was because we were on edge, one cannot tell, but all their movements - stuck as were in the very middle of our area - seemed purposeless and furtive, and very soon we began to shoot first and to ask questions afterwards. The I.O. began to rake them in to a sort of "black-hole", and even brought in a baby in arms, which seemed to be rather overdoing it.

At last near midday our attention was directed to something more serious. A report suddenly came in from "A" Company that they could see movement below the ridge due east of Point 172, and then another - very little later - that the enemy were forming up to attack.

The attack went in as they had expected, but it was hardly likely to be successful; the Bren and the 36 Grenade are much too deadly customers when they can be used down a steep jungle hillside. And once again the artillery was brought down to finish off the good work. This sort of thing did not worry us. It was an attempt at infiltration that we feared.

But the Jap hates to fail. If he does, you can be almost sure his mind will become a blank to every other alternative. And so it happened in this case. Once more the telephone rang. "They're still there," reported the company commander. "I can see them milling about like hell." "Where, though?" we asked patiently. "Give us a map reference." It came back. We rang up Brigade to ask what they could do. Was there any possibility of an air strike? It seemed a grand opportunity with the Japs crammed along the bottom of that ridge.

To our surprise a strafe was promised in half an hour, and we fiddled impatiently as the minutes went slowly by. The company commander kept ringing up. "How much longer now?".....". .still milling about. ..".....".can't think what they're up to; it's the chance of a life time....." It was like waiting for the dentist's chair. But the R.A.F. was not going to let us down. Close on the half-hour we could hear the Hurricanes in the distance, and then suddenly they were over us making their preliminary circle in the sky.

Pilots ought to know what it feels like to troops on the ground. One moment we were very much all on our own in the game, and then for a few blessed moments we were the spectators, with no responsibility and there just to enjoy ourselves. They wasted no time. Down each one would swoop from line astern towards the green ridge, and then with a noise like tearing sailcloth its cannon would open up and the dust spurted up beneath it. We had ten minutes of noise and snarling power and then with a last dip of their wings, the aircraft sped away with a tuneful hum into the distance.

The telephone tinkled and the receiver crackled while a group pressed eagerly around it. The Japs had disappeared from sight, but for a long time later they could be heard digging fresh graves and dragging away the groaning wounded. Between enfilade small arms fire and the guns and now aircraft, they must have been beginning to feel a bit sorry for themselves, though we hardly realized it at the time. The sun moved imperceptibly across the sky and in the still afternoon air the rumble at the ferry behind us went on. If there were always details to absorb as at headquarters, there was nothing for the men to do but watch and talk and count the time.

We felt worried about "172". If the Japs were nibbling at it so early, it gave them plenty of time and to probe and press elsewhere, and the position could not protect the left flank completely. There was nothing to prevent the enemy sneaking further round through the hills and then filtering down from the north along the banks of the Pi Chaung. We had no wire at all. There was still nothing to prevent them breaking through the centre, at least once it was dark. There was therefore a lot of reconnaissance to be done for new positions, closer to the river, to be taken up by night, and the villagers and snipers still kept a few men busy and the rest of us still very much on the alert.

Nothing had been done throughout the afternoon or evening so that our intentions should not be disclosed, but as soon as night fell there was a furious outbreak of activity. Loads were packed up and dumps were formed, and the two ferry crossings were prepared and marked. The withdrawal was timed to begin at 0200 hours and the guides had to be given their instructions and sent off to their companies. "B" and "D" Companies moved back to new positions, and "C" Company took up theirs in an arc to the north of Battalion Headquarters, which extended from the river bank to the edge of the village. Only "A" Company remained in their position at Point 172.

As the night passed we were beginning to hope that the Japs had had enough, but it was wishful thinking. Not very long after dark they attacked 172 again and then their attacks were repeated several times with great determination. The telephone kept ringing, and for a time all seemed well, but then another message came through.
"Its getting pretty hot here," the company commander reported. "Jim cant get back to his platoon. They're surrounded and ......". Then the line went dead.

It seemed a case for rather drastic measures, and the C.O. called for the gunner.
"Put the stuff down as close as you dare," he ordered. "We'll have to take the risk."
The gunner moved away quickly to the set and then loomed up again almost immediately, obviously rather crestfallen. "My own line's out," he whispered, "and there's not a bloody squeak on the R/T." This, when the firing on 172 had reached its highest pitch.

Our luck was in though. Furious with rage, the C.O. snatched the phone to Brigade and found that the Battery Commander was actually listening in. The Brigade line to the guns had just reeled in too, but he had a jeep and ploughed his way off through the mass of men converging on the bridgehead. The story he told later was amusing. Shouting as he drove right into the gun-line, he brought his jeep to rest by the G.P.O's mosquito net. "What's that?" asked the G.P.O., sticking his head out from under the net, but not waiting for a reply. "Ten rounds gunfire!" Only then did he ask for the target, to find that he was on the right line.

The shells whistled across our front and awoke the echoes around "172" for five minutes or more, and when they stopped there was complete silence. Half an hour later the company commander himself walked in to report that the coast was clear.

We were now beginning to feel desperately tired. With everything packed we could only sit in the darkness with nothing to do but keep awake. Midnight passed and then one o'clock, and the last hour was upon us with everybody praying that we should be allowed to move in peace. At 0145 hours a whisper in the darkness indicated that the boats had arrived. Would I see the Staff Captain, please, on the opposite bank? At 0158 hours the last details were settled and I started across the river to battalion headquarters, and then at two o'clock *exactly* a deafening outburst of fire shattered the silence within a hundred yards of the crossing place. Grenades exploded and red tracer flamed and criss-crossed across the sky. This was the last straw.

However the firing stopped. Nobody has since been able to tell whether it was a real or imaginary scare, but at the time it was just too much for the unarmed carriers, and some of them bolted. It made us very angry at the time, though we could hardly blame them. As we found later, they were prepared to stay anywhere provided they had some sort of weapon which would fire.

This was the end of "Cox's Corner", as the General later named it. It was a success, though it might easily have ended in disaster. But there must always be an element of luck in a battle, and in defence there is probably some tendency to underestimate the effectiveness of one's own efforts. Possibly this is most so in jungle warfare, where results are so difficult to see. The force opposing us had certainly been considerably stronger than our own, but it had lacked close support and - as the Japanese so often do - it persisted in attacking the strong points instead of seeking for, and exploiting the weak.

We learned later infact, from captured documents, that the casualties we caused were very high and that a few days later one of the units, badly shaken, had had to be withdrawn in order to recover from its losses.

The rest of the night was a strain, but we were left in peace. While the folding boats crept back and forth across the blue-black water, the village on the west bank slowly filled up as guides pushed sleepy men into the bestavail able cover, and harassed officers and N. C.O's hissed to keep them silent now that the tension was breaking. Into deserted houses we crept now and again to smoke cigarettes which all of us had longed for since darkness fell, and as the dawn broke and the last boat came across in misty sunlight, the smoke curled upwards from among the trees, as peacefully as at a picnic, and the prospect of hot tea made it seemed that our troubles were really over.

Appendix 'A'

LONG DISTANCE PATROL

By Major H. Olszewski, Polish Army.

"B" COMPANY 5 G. C. R.

"Here comes another task - hell if it's a patrol." That was the usual remark I uttered whenever a Battalion H.Q. runner approached my platoon. As I study the message ordering me to contact headquarters immediately, my platoon sergeant comes hurrying up and exclaims, "Say, what's up, another dirty job, sir?"
"Here we are again", I say.

We are not particularly fond of patrols; that can only be understood by one who is a familiar with the Burmese jungle. Our Africans also preferred to go in and attack Jap positions rather than go patrolling. But in the search for their hideouts, everyone had to do his share. And a very straining and tiring share it was too.

On march 11, 1944, I received a similar message from B.H.Q. - the second in three days - little realizing that this was going to be a pretty tough job. After giving orders to my platoon sergeant, I went along with my orderly. There I was met by the I.O. who said, "Sorry Henry, another sticky job for you". His briefing took about half an hour, and the further he went, the less I liked it. Our Division at that time was withdrawing as the Japs had effected movements intending to by-pass and set a block between the Division and its objective. Our own forces were in position on the right bank of the Pi Chaung and, according to reports, about 1,200 Japs were already moving north between the Pi Chaung and the Kaladan valley.

My job was to cross the river, ascertain the enemy moves and, if in contact with small parties of Japs, to give them all I had. Further, I was to report on the possibility of building jeep tracks to the Kaladan River. The trace given me was about 25 miles by the map, and in practice about 40 miles. To accomplish my task I had to probe along a circle from the Pi Chaung to the south east, then to the Kaladan, turning north, and back from the north-east to the battalion position. Apart from my British Sergeant, I had 34 Africans together with a 48-Set and a radio operator, and there were two carriers for the batteries. Three extra ammunition loads were taken, and four days rations were carried on each man.

When I passed on the news to the men, they took it calmly. "We do go, Akwey Allah", they shouted, meaning "we will do it, the Lord is in the heavens". Though that determination on the part of the Africans was encouraging, only my European sergeant and I realized what a jam we might get in. The Japs were as quick off the mark as we were.

At 1600 hours I began crossing the river under cover given by a platoon of "C" Company. The crossing was not pleasant as Jap patrols were caught and fired on two days before on the opposite bank of the river, and it was obvious we were now giving them their turn. We crossed in native canoes, eight men at a time across a chaung one hundred yards wide. The first crossing included myself and a party with two L.M.Gs. We hurriedly took up position to cover the crossing of the rest of the platoon, completed without incident in an hour. I had almost an hour of daylight left, so I decided to get as far as possible from the river.

By nightfall we had secured favourable high ground from which I could observe tracks running north and south on either side of the hill. Great caution was taken to maintain silence, especially in moment among huge, dry teak leaves which densely covered the hill. I ordered the wireless operator to get on the set, and he was soon in touch with B.H.Q.

All appeared quiet, until about 2300 hours, when sentries spotted strong Jap parties moving on the track west of our position. The information was immediately passed on the air to headquarters - "Baskets moving north, strength about one company plus Burmese coolies carrying loads". At about 0030 hours another party of Japs, of the same strength, were reported approaching us, and rather curiously stopped to rest at the very foot of my position. We could hear them talking among themselves, others coming as far as my forward position and within five yards, seeking spots to answer the call of nature. Everyone was tense and alert, swearing at the dry leaves which threatened to betray us.

We had also to reinforce our watch on Sergeant Carpenter's personal servant, whose snoring at nights would echo through the valleys. But tonight his friends took great care by tying a tring around his wrist and tugging it as soon as he began to snore. None of us, except he, had a wink of sleep, and at dawn we had to be on our way again. We had to cross open paddy just before daybreak, and up in the hills ahead we could observe smoke which we later found to be the remains of a fire lit by the Japs for breakfast.

Our first leg was reached at about 1400 hours in a village called Letpan. The village had been deserted, but there were signs of a recent Jap visit. From Letpan we started moving north-east and at 1800 hours, after a tiring march, coupled with the sleeplessness of the previous night, we made our harbour. Contact with Battalion H.Q. on the 48-Set was interrupted by unknown static, probably Japs, and we were asked who we were. We spent a quite night but for the sound of gunfire from our previous night's position and the noise of Pompin's snoring. Being so tired we hardly minded either.

Next day, the thirteenth, we started on our second leg for a place called Orama, situated on the banks of the Kaladan. Shortly after we moved, we came across a party of five Japs with a train of more than thirty coolies. They suddenly got wind of us, running into the jungle and abandoning their loads. The loads were mostly captured kit and medical equipment of our 29 C.C.S., who were attacked two weeks earlier. As we could not possibly carry the kit, it was burnt. The coolies we captured could not give much information about the Japs, as neither of us could understand the other language. But judging by the signs they made, I learnt a little about Jap dispositions.

At noon we reached Orama, where the villagers were helpful and willing to offer us petty aids. To interrogate them we had to drag them from their dugouts, where most of the villagers were still hiding from the enemy. We knew from past experience that this was a sign that the Japs were near, but we were able to leave Orama and harbour two miles further north without incident.

Having had nothing hot to eat or drink since we left the battalion area, we now lit fires for the first time in a deep chaung, and the boys prepared a meal of bully-beef stew. With biscuits and hot tea, it made us feel a lot better. It was like so many other patrols: intense effort and exhausting alertness all the time, with little chance for food or rest.

We tried again to get in touch with B.H.Q., but this time there was no answer. Another night passed without incident and at dawn we were on our way again. We took a guide from this village of Lasaung and moved across the same range of hills that we had crossed two days earlier, but this time many miles further north.

We had passed through a small village, when we heard shouting and a man came running towards us. He was an African, the sole survivor of the East African patrol which was ambushed when crossing the Kaladan a fortnight before. He had been living in the village, hoping to join an African unit. Each time troops approached the village the villagers had hidden him until they had found out who they were. They had successfully hidden him several times from the Japs, and we were the first friendly troops to come that way.

Before he left the village, the inhabitants insisted on his sharing the last meal with them, and then with farewell shouts we pushed on.

The Pi Chaung was now quite close, and we heard heavy firing in front, but when we reached the river bank at five in the afternoon opposite the battalion area, we found that the troops had gone. In defensive positions we again tried to make contact on the 48-Set, but without success. After a ten hours march through the hills, we felt unbelievably tired, and only the thought that we should soon rejoin had kept us going.

After a short conference we decided to push on towards the noise of battle, hoping for the best. Luck was with us, for we crossed the river some way further north at dusk and about 2000 hours were nearly shot up by one of our own platoons.

We had long been given up for lost and our welcome was one of the heartiest I have ever experienced.

There was nothing spectacular about the patrol except the marching and the hills we had to climb and the constant probability of running into forces far stronger than our own. Little happened here, but it was often more of a relief when something did.

CHAPTER VII

"THE KYRINGI LOOP"

IT is probably true to say that no one had remained unperturbed by the events near "Iraq." So much might have happened; the Japs might have secured Cox's Corner; they might have pressed strongly from the south and seriously have hampered the crossing of the bridge; they might have used artillery with deadly effect on the narrow bottleneck, or in any part of the open plain which we had had to cross. Coming as it did immediately after the forced marches in our advance, both officers and men were nearing a state of exhaustion, and the consequences of a hard fought rear-guard action might have been serious. The Africans too were openly bewildered and, as in most hasty withdrawals where changes of plan are ineviable, the majority of the junior European ranks had an exaggerated picture of the situation.

Under the circumstances the Divisional Commander reached the conclusion that it was essential, as soon as possible, to secure a "Box" a good deal further north where the many casualties, who had all to be carried on men's heads, could be safely evacuated by air, and all ranks could be given a period of rest and recuperation. The situation then would fall naturally into its true perspective. The decision was obviously a wise one, though 5 G. C. R. had hoped an easier passage once the river was crossed. Instead we continued our forced marches northwards for a further three days, once again over miles of dusty paddy, while 6th Brigade conducted the rear-guard action against the pursuing but cautious 55th Cavalry. We were so tired that there were signs of carelessness, but luck was with us and nothing happened.

The Japanese 55th Cavalry Regiment had been our oppenents in all the actions we had fought on our way south and we had already begun to regard them as rather peculiar friends and to speak of them as "old 55 Cav." We could not help admiring their skill in springing surprises, their amazing ability to conceal themselves, their quickness, daring and bravely. They fought cleanly and there was at least one occasion when it is certain they held their fire until a squad of stretcher bearers were past.

It was said that the older and more disciplined units had practically never been known to indulge in atrocities, though their treatment of prisoners was harsh from one point of view. Trained as they were to exist for lengthy periods at almost starvation level, it is not surprising that they lacked sympathy for those captured, particularly as they had also been trained to regard a prisoner as the lowest form of life. Possibly, too, there is some justification for certain cases in which wounded men were bayonetted without mercy, for a wounded Jap will never regard himself as helpless, and so he may expect us to have the same point of view. There was a case in which a wounded Japanese prisoner was asked if he did not fear ill-treatment, and his answer was interesting, though it may prove nothing. "No", he replied boldly. "I expect to be treated in the same way as we treat our own prisoners."

The method of defence known as the "Defensive Box" had recently been used by the 7th Indian Division on the main front, where the Jap right hook towards Taung Bazaar and the Goppe Pass had just been foiled. It had not been used before in Burma on such a large scale and the Press made great play with the expression. It was however exactly the same in principle as the Harbour which we had adopted on a battalion level ever since our campaign started, and was the natural method which a formation would use which has no L. of C. and is supplied by air. The only difference in our method at that time was that we invariably secured all the surrounding high ground, while having the level areas free for medical and administrative units, and for the air dropping site. This might leave actual physical gaps in the perimeter, but we knew that the enemy always went for the highest ground and for the thickest cover, and he would be an easy target if he changed his tactics.

It was after more than three days marching northwards that the 81st Division adopted its first box, covering an abrupt and almost completed loop of the Pi Chaung some five miles east of the Kaladan. Inside the straight western edge of this loop it was decided to build our Dakota strip, and here we should receive our first reinforcements, replenish the heavy stores and fly out the wounded. There were no such things as Bulldozers to level out the ground, but Africans with picks and shovels, carrying small baskets of earth on their heads, can alter the face of the countryside in a very short time. In a few days the big aircraft came gliding in great clouds of dust to pick up the men and bear them away to safety. There was no more for us to do but to secure the loop and to maintain the continuous vigilance of our patrol.

The effect of our stay was like that of a boiling bath taken after a strenuous game of rugger. It enabled one's mind and body to rest and recuperate. For the first time for weeks, it seemed, we could bathe, wash, and mend our clothes in peace; play cards, visit our friends and catch up with the big arrears of mail.

But the enemy remained in contact. There always seemed to be something going on. One might wake up any night to the sound of some brief fusillade in the distance, or lie in bed at every dawn listening to the inevitable crackle of some medium machine guns which the Japs moved around assiduously from point to point. There were frequent patrol crashes, and the enemy also had some guns dropping a shell or two every day in the area of the airfield or of our own batteries. Day after day the impudent Hurricanes could be seen diving down to tree level in their efforts to detect movement, and our batteries would open up on their information or that of some patrol, just came in. But it was peace, nevertheless. Even with our slight experience, it was possible to tell at once, when firing broke out, whether we were effected or not, and there was an undoubted, if selfish, sedative effect in realizing that some other unit was holding the baby. It is one of the blessings of the human character, perhaps, that the sound of firing in another area never conjures up visions of casualties etc., but that only that just something is going on from the military or tactical point of view.

For all the periods of comparative peace, however, which we experienced from time to time, the arduousness of the long-range penetration role on which we were employed should be borne in mind. In the dense jungles there could never be said to be a moment during which contact could be considered definitely broken and unlike other formations, there was also no chance with us of being taken back into reserve. There was also the big factor that we had not even a third brigade by which the changes could be rung. It was a case of "some action", without a break, for a period of six months.

For the staffs and services, and for the most senior officers in battalion, the phase in the Kyringi Loop was one of almost complete relaxation, but it was a completely different matter for the platoon or patrol commander. There could never be any relaxation in the matter of patrolling, and the jungle patrol is both physically and mentally wearing. It was always an inspiration to witness the cheerful willingness of these brave leaders, and depressing to notice their vitality slowly fading and their faces growing drawn and thin. As the campaign went on their sickness rate rose rapidly beyond that of the others, but it subtracted nothing from the opinion I had formed as to the incredible resistance and endurance of the human body.

The Japs, judging by documents captured later, can be accused of wishful thinking at this period. They appeared to be fully under the impression that we were in full flight, and that we were unlikely to stop before reaching the Indian frontier. They used expressions such as "beaten enemy", "remnants","scattered forces", and they sent out units no bigger than platoons and sections, which were rather surprised to find that they were dealing with battalions and brigades. Our forces at Kyringi were some 10,000 - 12,000 more than their estimates. As a result they came in for some pretty rough handling now and again.

On one occasion the 55 Cav. Headquarters and some other troops, having found nothing further north, walked unexpectedly into the forward company of the 7th Battalion (Gold Coast) at night. They became completely disorganized, but - typical of the Japs - attacked furiously just the same. Even their medical orderlies joined in. It was also typical that they succeeded in penetrating the position, but then the C.O. made a bold decision and the 7th's mortars were brought down on their own forward area. As a result the enemy suffered very heavily and no less than four of their much coveted officers' swords were borne in triumphantly when dawn broke.

It was at Kyringi that the 1st. Battalion (Sierra Leone), very skilfully and very gallantly, captured the guns which had harassed us for so many days, and that one of our own companies on patrol was attacked and surrounded and drove off the Japs with the bayonet. But perhaps the most inspiring effort at that time was that of an African wireless operator, whose O.P. had been attacked and over-run. "We are being attacked", he reported calmly to Battery H.Q. "The officer has been killed. I think the position will be captured. Shall I come in?" "O.K." was the reply. "Come in now. Destroy the set before you leave." There was then a pause while the noise of the firing couldbe clearly heard in the earphones at Battery Headquarters. Then the operator's voice came up again. "Wilco" it said. "Hallo, hallo! I can give you a target. Here it is." And he carefully gave the reference. "Coming in now." All the others in the O.P. were killed, except two, but as a result of the African's coolness the target was very successfully dealt with.

It was necessary. during the time we had to spare in the Box, to make adjustment to some of our ideas and to absorb some of the more important lessons. There was food for thought. We were beginning to learn, I believe, that speed was not everything - far from it - particularly in the jungle. We had seen the effect on the troops of over-taxing the physical capabilities, in failing to explain the full and true situation as it developed from moment to moment. We were sure by then that every African *must* have firearms, even if he never uses them. We knew that against the Japs, the first to secure the highground, however impenetrable, is in the stronger position every time.

But it was in the matter of leadership, at least among the Africans, that there arose the most interesting reflections. It seemed here that the outward efficiency and drive, to which so much respect is paid, was by no means among the first among a leader's assets. Some of the best of these were inefficient in comparison with others and lacking in knowledge; some of them had nothing to gain by their appearance. They were normally tolerant and broad-minded but often appeared easy going until the moment for action arrived. But it seemed to me that the greatest asset of all the best leaders was their sense of anticipation. Such a large number of officers and N.C.Os. seemed to lack this completely. To them the situation was merely that which presented itself at the moment. They lacked a sense of suspicion, and usually failed to consider more than the outcome of their own plans. To them there were practically no "Possibilities"; it was all a matter of "Probables". It seemed to be their difference in this respect that made the real leader. Apparently this was obvious to men, so that their confidence was immeasurably increased, and it seemed to *be* confidence and the consequent feeling of security - of being looked after - which meant more to the African than anything else

So we recuperated; letter writing, reading, arguing after supper at night; sometimes playing cards, luxuriating in an occasional afternoon nap under the shady trees. The office staffs had their first opportunity to catch up with correspondence and returns. There were pay question- to be sorted out: clothing and equipment was repaired and exchanged, and defaulters were enabled to reflect gloomily on the foolishness of their past misdeeds. One might hear hymns from under shady trees as the padres made their rounds, or a few rounds of distant rifle fire: while all day long, it seemed, the Dakotas roared over our heads to drop their coloured parachutes, and the 'Moths' sputtered off from the airfield with a wounded man or someone newly sick. Everyday there were working parties to be found and some new improvement to the defences to be carried out. There were calls to conferences, reconnaissances to be made, patrols briefed, but for all that we began to grow restless. Rumours were rife.

At last the General himself made the situation clear to us. One day he made a complete tour of all the units in the Division to tell us we had one main operation to come before we went out to rest. He ended up very flankly. "You are improving." He told us, "but you are not yet soldiers." And he put his monocle to his eye to survey us.

"Very green, in fact", he ended, though not unkindly. It was easy enough, he went on, when a force was rapidly advancing - everything looked after itself. The real test came when the enemy got the upper hand. Or appeared to get it. It was then that leadership came in, and you had to pay attention to men's minds, as well as their bodies and weapons. "Any difficulties you may have had," he said in conclusion, "arose out of failure to do that." Which we knew was true.

It was chastening but good, but I feel a mistake was made in telling us that there was but one other operation to be done. "One more show," the General had said. "And then out!" From that very moment you could feel the pressure drop.

The Regular Soldier may have learnt that no military forecast is ever a promise, and that even a promise can quite often not be carried out, but even after four or five years this fact is still a puzzle to the more civilian minds. In this instance we lost quite a lot of prestige among the Africans because, not only this, but other forecasts could not be adhered to.

The reasons for our preliminary move from Kyringi once again to Kaladan were various. At Taung Bazaar the Japanese counter-stroke had ended in failure, but it had caused much delay, and for this and other reasons, connected with the European theatre, it had now been decided that the move on Akyab by XV Corps could not be completed before the Monsoon. At the same time it would be quite impossible for the bulk of the forces employed in the coastal belt to remain among the flooded paddy fields, and it was essential that this thinning out process should not be disorganized by further flank attacks. Our role, therefore, was to contain as a large a force as possible in the Kaladan Valley up to the middle of April, when it would be safe for us to withdraw slowly across to the main front to make our own exit.

Actually the enemy in the Kaladan were far more intent on cutting our own L. of C. than in interfering with the Arakan operations. Their appreciation was that we must either return by West African Way or abandon our guns and M.T. altogether. The so-called 'Soutcol' route, which ran from the area of Kaladan Village to the Kalapanzin Valley, was no more than a rough track, and could never be made motorable in the time available; and the Japs knew that there were no other passes, North or South, other than the one by which we had come. It was estimated that at least two Jap battalions were hurrying northwards to achieve this object and, although a battalion of Punjabis had been brought down quickly to meet this threat, it was considered unlikely that the guns could be got away unless at least a part of the Division could be sent to support them. It would be a close thing, but there was confidence that it could be done.

Slowly the Division began to thin out from the Kyringi area, constructing a new section of the jeep track as they went, and once again we made our way up and over the precipitous hills and on to the banks of the Kaladan. The General's intention was first, of course, to get the guns away, but he proposed to "take a good crack" at the Japs in the process. 6th Brigade were to cross the river for this task, while we in 5th Brigade had the job of clearing the area of Kaladan Village and then of co-operating in harrying the Japs on the far side of the river. The guns in the meantime would slip northwards on the west bank of the river, crossing to the east when they were behind the Punjabis.

It should be mentioned here that a great deal of the information we received during the campaign, and in this particular instance, was obtained through an organization known as "V Force," which was formed after the retreat from Burma 1942. In all the operational areas it had its sections, led by British Officers, whose job often kept them working many miles behind the enemy's lines.

"V Force" was sometimes the subject of somewhat unkind remarks. The Japs were supposed to have a similar organization, and it was often said that some of the agents worked for both sides. Nevertheless the information they gave us was usually remarkable accurate and very valuable, and it can easily be imagined under what dangerous conditions it was obtained, for there were certainly collaborators among the Burmese who were quite prepared to betray their own countrymen to the Japs. Many burnt our villages and deserted farms tell the tale of Jap reprisals for information given away, and it was rather sad and humiliating to us to know that yet for another lengthy period we should now be compelled to leave these friendly people to their mercy.

Some of the main criticisms about "V. Force" information was that it was always too late, that it was often just a guess; that its estimates of numbers could at least be divided by four. Yet there were always plenty of volunteers anxious to join them. Their difficulties were not realized. In the first place messengers often had to travel four or five days from their report centre, and it was impossible to travel loaded - in a country swept bare of food - for fear of rousing suspicion. Thus they had to sneak from village to village by night, relying entirely on the hospitality extended to them.

Their worst difficulty, though was the Jap propensity for splitting up its forces into tiny packets far and wide. There were no rules by which to expect his presence. One might meet a patrol, or a foraging party, an ambush or an O.P. Odd soldiers had the habit of appearing on every known and unknown track, often without any apparent reason, and on many occasions the Japs deliberately laid out a broad system of picquets when they knew that agents were working in an area. It could hardly be surprising then that information given *was* often rather late, but at least it gave a picture of the situation, a living atmosphere; and it was still possible to make accurate deduction, in spite of that, as to probable moves and intentions.

Our experience of V Force reports was that on many occasions they could tell you the almost exact position of a gun or an enemy ambush, or the habits of Jap patrols. In the more open coastal areas they often led patrols of our Reconnaissance Regiment to the very house where Japs were quartered, and it was possible for men to gain almost complete patrol ascendancy in that way. The romance of it was always striking when one came suddenly face to face with one of the little parties, hurrying practically defenceless along some winding jungle path, or when one came across one of their officers sitting cheerfully in a village clearing away out in the blue.

At this particular time V. Force information was that the Japs had a small force in Kaladan village with other detachments in the hills to the north west and south west of that area. 5th Brigade's plan to send the 8th Battalion (Gold Coast) to the norh west, leaving one of their companies and one of 5 G.C.R. at Sigtaung, may seem simple enough - the main body was to proceed to the river to press northwards through Ngame - but it was not an easy problem. It meant that both the detached forces would have to take their air-supply drops in the most unsuitable areas. They would have no means of evacuating casualties and, in addition, at that time the water supply points were getting short and widely separated.

A detached company was always a headache. It seemed to be the occasion for a wireless set to be dropped down a hillside, and the party which had to be sent struggling over the hills with a replacement could so easily be ambushed and destroyed by some intervening Jap patrol.

All went well on this occasion, however. 8 G.C.R. filed off into the hills, and we in 5 G.C.R., who where performing both flank and rear-guard duties, trailed comfortably behind the main brigade column. For the first time in the campaign the battalion was in Brigade reserve and it conjured up pretty ideas wherein we sat listening to other people's battles and criticised their tactics when the evening "Sitreps" came in. Later on we learnt to distrust the task most heartily, for it always seemed to be the prelude to the most energetic piece of work we had yet done.

From the moment when we reached Ngame on the Kaladan we were never still. On the first night our task was to guard "the back door", but Brigade discovered gaps and next morning two of the companies had to be moved to new positions. After that - just south of Grankhazi - 7 G.C.R. made contact and their two reserve companies had to be moved forward. This again altered the shape of the Brigade box, so once more we moved. Next a report came in from the detachment south-west of Kaladan; the enemy had been bumped in strong positions near the little of Atawn North. So we were to make a reconnaissance at once and clear up the place as soon as possible.

One would prefer to draw a veil over the whole of the next period. The country seemed to be the most broken and the most formless that we had yet come across. It took two aching hours with binoculars and stereoscope to decide which route there was likely to be the least impossible of them all. It then took me eight hours and the 2 i / c five hours each to reach and reconnoitre just a small part of the area we expected to use: and then it was only possible even to see the objective at nothing less than a mile. We then had to struggle back down boulder-strewn chaungs in order to plan most of the night for a move which, at all costs, must be completed the next day. We duly completed it, but only to find that the birds had flown, and then - for reasons that need not to be recorded - we moved and counter-moved until everyone was exhausted. It had been a hot and sultry day, but when at last it was possible to call a halt the best water to be found was a stagnant pool, beside which lay the body of a decomposing Japanese officer. Nevertheless we determined to stay where we were. If the tea would have to be more heavily chlorinated, at least it would be tea.

Every Englishman is aware of his propensity for tea, but none of us is so aware of its sheer necessity until he goes on active service. Provided we had our tea, everything else could wait. We could do without food, if necessary, and resign ourselves to filthy clothes or the streaming rain, so long as the blessed tea was forthcoming. To dig in quickly as soon as a column reached harbour was, we knew, the first essential, but the fire and the tea-kettle almost shared that priority. It was a ritual. No casual visit was made and no conference was begun without it. Its arrival would bring a smile to the face of a tired man and quite visible relief to the wounded, and if there were ever people at home who cavilled at their meagre ration they may gain some consolation in the knowledge that many a worn out soldier has managed to keep going on their sacrifices.

However we were to get no tea this day. It never rains but it pours - that truest of sayings. Our heavy equipment had only just been flung tiredly on the ground; weary boys with matchets were just making up their minds to clear the best areas they could find for their masters' beds; "chop" loads, as people went about their duties, were being eyed thankfully as they at last came safely in; defence sections filed by to their posts; the signallers had already begun to set up their instruments and the welcome blue smoke had just begun to curl upwards through the trees, when the message came through which dashed all our suppressed longings to the ground.

It was the Brigade Major on the phone, and he was decently apologetic.
"There has been a rather unexpected turn in the situation," he said. "How soon can you move?" It appeared that the ferry which was being prepared at Ngame had been attacked the previous night by a mixed force of Japs and I.N.A.
"At the moment there's only a company of the Gambie's there", he went on. "And a few odds and sods. Can you get at least another company there by nightfall."

I handed over the battalion to the 2 i/c and, with the leading company commander and two orderlies hurrried back to the ferry. Our long detour, starting soon after dawn, had cut us off from the new atmosphere which now prevailed as we dodged our way past sweating load carriers and resting groups of chattering Africans towards the air strip. The restful days of the Kyringi Loop were obviously over. We could hear short bursts of small arms fire away to the south and, from the cover of the hills on our right, the dull "plop" of the 7th Battalion's mortars throwing their bombs into Grankhazi.

At the far end of the air strip a louder bang made us think at first that our guns were also in action, but when a truck appeared round the corner driven with unusual rapidity and no consideration whatever for other road - users we realized that it must have been the burst of a Japanese mortar. There was blood on the track and we negotiated that corner as rapidly as dignity would allow. Then we reached the village and came upon the A. D. S. underneath the trees. There were nearly a dozen wounded there, lying mainly on their faces, with gaping red slashes in their dark skins; some of them almost as big as the palm of the hand and obviously mortar wounds. They were so quiet and calm that they might have been on a medical inspsection.

At the river bank we discovered that the mortar was firing from about a mile up-stream. Nobody could spot him, but he could obviously see us, for we were forced to leap into a convenient slit-trench three times in as many minutes, and a party of sappers had to run for cover, leaving two of their dead by the water side.

The mortar can be a most disturbing weapon. It goes off with such an innocent pop, but there is no indication how safe you are from the moment you hear the ugly whisper overhead until the bomb lands with a very loud crash, sometimes on top of you and sometimes as much as two hundred yards away.

Obviously this particular part of the bank was unsuitable for a crossing, even though the mortar now turned its attention to the A.D.S. We spotted the officer in charge of the ferry further down and made our way back through the village to meet him.

There was very little to be arranged. The boats were ready, and covered approaches had already been cut through the elephant grass, which ran down the bank from the village. As we waited for the company to come along, we sat eating handfulls of sugar to quell the groaning emptiness inside us and thought about tea. Then the troops arrived and work began again.

By 2130 hours the men were across the river, disposed in foxholes. The defences were a bit thin but at least we had the light battery to support us. The 22 Set had got touch with Brigade and the musical rhythm of the rapid morse came up to us from the depths of a native dug-out. From across the river came the news that the battalion was harboured for the night. After fifteen hours of solid movement we had it seemed at last come to rest.

There had been so much to attend to during and after our crossing that by morning the enemy mortar had slipped our memories. It had in fact ceased to fire after its last disastrous salvo into the A.D.S. It was therefore rather a shock to us when it opened up again after such a peaceful night, especially since it had changed position and could now fire right into the embarkation point. A fair number of men had managed to cross before it was fully light, but then the mortar quickly got the range of all the likely forming-up places. One crowded boat received a direct hit, and though the battery searched all the most likely spots, they had not enough ammunition to spare, and the Japs insolently continued to fire. So we had again to move the crossing point out of range.

This was not to be our lucky day. Not far below the village the river bent sharply to the South West, which caused the shifted ferry crossing to come into full view of that reach of the river. It was probably quite by chance that the Japs had posted some machine guns at the far end of it, but once again the troops in the boats came under fire - a perfect example of 'out of the frying pan ......'

Although the water was being whipped up all around them, there were no casualties. If there had been, it would have been a different matter, but as it was, while we stood on the opposite bank, we had our best laugh for a long time.

It was a typically African scene. From their orderly course the boats at once broke formation, and there was a wild dive for cover behind the frail canvas sides of the boats. Then, by some amazing feat of contortion, their paddles reappeared over the sides of the boats, furiously to thrash the water. In some of the boats all the paddles appeared on one side only, while in others they thrashed in opposite directions, the inevitable result being a series of the proverbial small circles in the very middle of the highly accurate but quite ineffective cone of fire. Furious arguments could be heard from nearly every boat, though no man could be seen, while in one of them a British sergeant, lived with rage, was plying his paddle on the backs of a reluctant crew with only a meagre amount of success.

Between fear and laughter we watched things slowly sort themselves out - as they always will - while frantic Europeans on either bank shouted furious threats and instructions. It was something of a feat that in the midst of it all the Company Commander managed to take an accurate bearing as he struggled across, and he came panting to report, it when he had got over. At the same time one of the mortar officers reported seeing movement in the same place, so that it was only a matter of a few minutes later that several of us saw the Japs dispersing frantically from the cloud of dust put up by our bursting 3.7s.

It was not expedient, however, to complete the crossing that day. Evidently the mortar had moved once again, and now it had the range of the whole beach. There was also some very accurate sniping, and since there was no great urgency, it did not seem worth while incurring casualties. But we sent off "C" Company to occupy a ridge running parallel with the river, a little way to the north of Kyauktan. This the "I" Staff had told us was already occupied by patrols of 6th Brigade. Once we got there in strength, it seemed, the enemy mortar would have to withdraw.

"C" Company quickly made contact, but not with 6th Brigade. The company commander, with a bullet through his hand, reported that the ridge was firmly held by at least a platoon of Japs, and that there were no signs there of our own patrols. (We learnt later that they were actually on it, but had seen no signs of the enemy, or us, in the thick jungle). The enemy had apparently sneaked in after the ridge had been reported clear, and calmly established their position between our two forces.

We learnt from that moment never to accept the reports of even our own patrols entirely; it had now been proved more than once that a force could pass another by yards and never know of its existence.

During the campaign there were several instances of this happening; of Japs with loads walking straight through a company position in the darkness, or being asked sleepily "Is that you Bill?" as one of them stumbled against a sleeping figure. Normally they got clean away with it, but on one occasion there was great indignation - rather misplaced - because an officer rudely awakened the surrounding sleepers by shooting a Jap through his mosquito net. It was not a case of cunning or super stealth on the part of the Jap but invariably because of his sheer ignorance that we were there. A planned or stealthy approach always seemed to be spotted by our sentries.

Our attack on the "200 Feature", as this ridge came to be known, again took us three days; it then had to be called off just as we were about to complete its capture. There was nothing distinguished about it, and if we had had thorough night training, it would have been easy enough to have captured it in the dark. It does serve, however, to illustrate one or two points; the first being that we had been given no clear cut objective to achieve on the east side of the river - of which everyone was aware. The second was that mortars and artillery, unless put down in exceptionally heavy concentrations which ensure direct hits on practically every foxhole, can be quite ineffective if an attack has to be made up an almost vertical hillside.

The guns on this occasion undoubtedly inflicted casualties for we could hear the screams of the wounded men, but in spite of this our attacks were quite easily repulsed. We were a battalion attacking a platoon but the approaches were so narrow that we could only attack with a platoon ourselves. We heard a story later in the year in which, so it was said, the shape of a hill had literally been changed by a furious artillery bombardment, yet the attacking troops were still met by heavy automatic fire when they came to make their assault.

It is not an easy matter to break off a battle at any time; much less so when it is near the end of a day and no previous warning has been given. It was a little demoralizing, therefore, later still on the third day, to learn that we were *also* expected to re-cross the river the same night. At 1600 hours, when this order came through, the battalion was dispersed in all directions. "B.H.Q." had been established on a round feature, a little south of "200", known as "Signal Hill"; "D" Company were attacking the southern tip of "200" from the rear, and

"B" were five hundred yards behind them; "C" Company were holding the east flank and supporting the attack with mortar fire; while the remaining company, the Auxiliary Group, Headquarters Company and the rear elements of BHQ were still in Kyauktan, five hundred south of Signal Hill.

Wearily the miles of telephone wire had to be reeled in; fresh orders were issued over the air, and a growling "Ack" despatched to Brigade Headquarters. Since the Japs were still there, and covering all the stretch of open ground to the east of "200", it was then necessary to make a wide detour through the hills before the battalion could be concentrated to the north. So after all our labour, and perhaps rather intricate planning, we were forced to fade away fro our prize in the gathering dusk, sped by the impudent parting shots of the triumphant Japs.

On all the occasions when we were to re-fight our battles in the future, the move that night was never otherwise spoken of than as "that perfectly bloody march". Our track, or to be more accurate, the route we took, wound for most of the way up a narrow, boulder strewn chaung. The hills on either side were somehow damp and depressing, and, as they closed in, every vestige of light disappeared. We tripped and stumbled, cursing softly in the darkness, and it was after very little of this that two of our stretcher cases begged to stop and thereafter preferred to walk. One of them had a badly sprained back, but his action surprised none. Only one small incident relieved the pervading depression for me. Rounding a bend past the dim crouching forms of the halted column, I ran into four "Aux-Group" carriers with - of all things - an assault boat rested beside them. At that point the track was but two feet wide and cut out of the side of a very steep slope; the boat was quite twice the width and about as unwieldy as it is possible to imagine. An officer stepped forward in the darkness.
"I doubt if we can get this much further", he apologised. "Do you think we might break it up?"
I thought of the way we had come: of the boulders, the walking stretcher cases, of my own tired feet and ill-temper. And I felt better. I signed to them and they began to cut it up. There was nothing to touch these African carriers.

Soon afterwards we panted up the last twenty feet to "B" Company's area on the top of "200". The company columns faded away with their guides, and we set about to form ourselves into some sort of order in the darkness. Black figures squeezed and stumbled past among the bamboos, and tired headloaders could be heard flinging their burdens to the ground. Within ten minutes an impatient voice from Brigade was on the set.
"What time can we expect you at the crossing?" It was two miles up the river.
What time!
It took a bit to make the situation quite clear. But staffs are reasonable whenever they can be, and they gave us permission to stop the night. They are perhaps more reasonable than one suspects at times, for tempers get short and tired fighting units are apt to imagine that they are the only people who do any work.

We slept that night in peace and made the return to our brigade without incident the following day.

6th Brigade's operations east of the Kaladan, and perhaps the threat of our move across the river at Kyauktan, had partly failed and partly succeeded. The time available was so limited the 6th Brigade had failed to destroy the main enemy force north of us, though the casualties they inflicted were quite satisfactory. But they prevented any further northward move by the Japs and so ensured that the guns and other transport were got away without interference. Once this was done our task in the Kaladan was complete, and the next move was to transfer the whole division across the hills, this time westwards into the valley of the Kalapanzin.

CHAPTER VIII

WESTWARDS, AND THE ACTION AT PYINGYAUNG.

DURING the brief operations of the 5th Gold Coast at Kyauktan the remainder of 5th Brigade and divisional headquarters had withdrawn slowly northwards from Ngame to Kaladan village, and another box had been formed around it. As a position in which a formation intended to stay put it left little to be desired, since the hills surrounding it were as steep and as difficult as any we had known, but as an area from which to sneak out unobserved it was far less suitable because the only two reasonable exits could easily have been completely blocked by quite a minor force. The few days we spent there was therefore rather an anxious period, for the Japs were very active and they had only to discover our true intentions to be sure to make our withdrawal a really awkward proposition. That they did not do so was due to their own wishful thinking and to General Woolner's careful plans.

The General calculated that the enemy were almost certain to imagine that we would withdraw along the jeep track, the way we had come. To give force to this probability he had opposed the crossings of the Mi Chaung, which ran into the Kaladan from the north east. Earlier in our withdrawal he had caused a bogus operation order to be left behind, showing our intention to move in this direction, and when the division eventually did move, he himself set off northwards with 6th Brigade and divisional headquarters in order to appear to confirm it. But 5th Brigade struck due west, and it was only when the main column had gone a long way north, taking dummy air drops on the way, that it suddenly changed direction and swung back to rejoin us.

The result was perfect. Only the 1st Gambia Battalion, supported by the Punjabis, withdrew slowly astride the jeep track, while the division moved away unopposed. The Japs, still intent on cutting off the guns, which had long since got away, faithfully followed the wrong scent.

The march westwards towards the main front was without incident, but in parts it was certainly one of the hardest we had yet done. It was made harder by the fact that we had to go without air supply in order to conceal our intentions, and each man carried five days rations in addition to his pack and his heavy head load. Through Kammang, where the 5th Gold Coast had made their first contact over three months before, the track ran on past Bidonegyaungywa, across the Pi Chaung, through Kalagya and then over the Romadaung Pass which was no less formidable than its name would suggest.

Few of us will forget that pass, which we reached at the very hottest time of the day. It was just under three thousand feet high, and on the upward slope we halted twice after unbroken forty-five minute periods of movement. I shall always remember it by the droplets of sweat from each marching man, which literally almost laid the dust and on which I fastened my fascinated attention in order to stop thinking about reaching the top.

From then on it was just foot-slogging, but never easy going for however strict the discipline, and no matter how careful the staff arrangements, the movement of some twenty thousand men in single file is almost certain to become a series of jerks and stops, which is far more tiring than steady movement in a march three times as long. It was also a move which followed watercourses almost entirely, crossing and re-crossing chaungs sometimes twenty times within a mile; clawing our way up steep banks of soft clay, made slippery by thousands of wet feet, or dragging forward with weighted clothing through knee-deep water for hundreds of yards at a time.

At Wagai, arriving long after dark, we threw ourselves down among grass which could cut like a knife and slept, heedless of the damp and the dirt of cows and buffaloes, completely tired out. On another occasion a company had to be left behind to picquet a flank, their rations being four boxes of grenades with which to catch fish - if there were any. And in the last stages

THE ACTION AT PYINGYAUNG

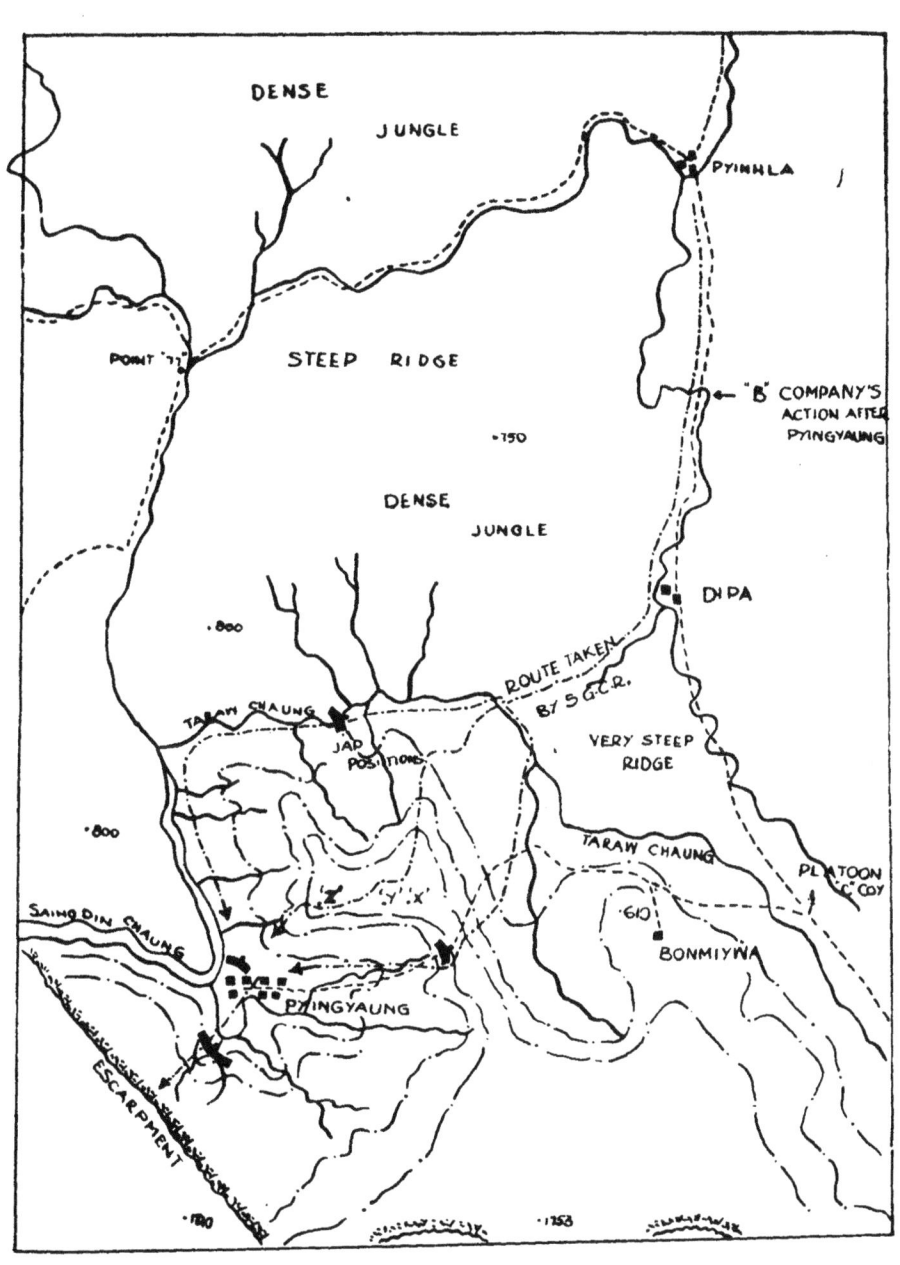

we picked our way endlessly along tiring narrow rock ledges above a broadening river, and in the hot afternoon sun looked down enviously into its waters at the shoals of fish which vanished maddeningly at every halt. We always seemed to be hungry. These calm reaches, not at all un-English if the bamboo were less evident, would have drawn holiday crowds on any summer day, but in the irritations of a divisional column on the move it was difficult really to appreciate it. We thought just of the next halt and of the next meal, and of the kind of place we would harbour in that night.

At Pyinhla the column at last halted to rest and to build a moth strip. Here a branch of our track forked south and south-west through Dipa, while other and lesser trails dropped down over the hills and joined it from the north. There were reports of Japanese and I.N.A. in the neighbourhood, and it was necessary to clear these approaches as alternatives fro our exit shortly in to the Kalapanzin valley.

The Battalion had expected to settle down here for at least four days rest, and we began the task of clearing the bamboo and digging ourselves in with the pleasant anticipation of letter writing, books and papers, and quiet evening chats over the glass of rum which was now a regular issue. But we were to be disappointed again. Along the north bank of the Saingdin Chaung the track ran on to Mazegyaung Khamwe, where a more suitable divisional harbour had been found. As it had not yet been decided by which route we should debouch onto the Kalapanzin there were three alternatives which had to be explored - the route continuing west along the chaung, a north-westerly route in the direction of Letpanywya, or the one to the south through Dipa. And this last was the job we now had to do.

Within thirty-six hours of our arrival the Brigadier gave us the situation so far as it was known. Dipa, he said, was unoccupied; but further south the locals reported conflictingly of Jap forces ranging between two hundred and a thousand strong. He showed on the map how the Dipa track broke to the north-west from Bonmiywa, divided there and then came together once more at Pyingyaung. This place, he suspected, was occupied, and since it lay on the south bank of the Saingdin Chaung it threatened any move which the division might wish to make along the most direct route to the Kalapanzin. Pyingyaung was to be our objective, and from there we were to report if the route westwards on the south side of the chaung could be made suitable for the move of the division.

The map showed that the track through Bonmiywa was narrow, twisting, easy to cut and lending itself everywhere to ambush, but from the air photographs it seemed that we might be able to strike across the hills south-west of Dipa and thereby shorten our L. of C. appreciably. Such a course might also achieve surprise, which would just make the difference, for the final approach to the village was so obvious that once our intention had been divulged the enemy would have little difficulty in delaying us for days. These approaches came into Pyingyaung at right angles to each other; one over the hills from the east and from the village of Bonmiywa, and the other following the Taraw Chaung westwards and then southwards down the banks of the Saingdin Chaung. In between this rectangle rose a broken hill feature with three pimples along its southern edge, from of at least one of which it seemed certain that we should get a good view of the objective and all the surrounding country. If we were to attack Pyingyaung from both north and east, it was essential that we ourselves should dominate the high ground between our split forces. Thus the plan was to move secretly into the Taraw Chaung and to seize these pimples, and then to explore the approaches to the village from all the most likely directions.

A platoon was sent ahead the night before to cut a track from Dipa south west across the hills, and early the next morning the main column set off. But it was soon held up. The track had been cut quite easily up to the top of the ridge, but it could be got no further. It was hard to believe that *no* way down could be found, but it was a fact, and the legs of philosophical Africans which one had to stumble over in the process of making sure, seemed to indicate cheekily that this ought to have been quite clear to us from the start.

You cannot normally send men down a near precipice with mortar barrels and ammunition boxes on their heads. Nevertheless we determined it must be done, or half the day would be wasted. So casting first one way and then the other, the men began to dig footholds into the stony slope with heels or matchets, clinging tightly to the bamboos as they slowly progressed. Bamboos were half cut and bent over so as to make rails or handholds and the work gathered way. The headloaders did not wait for orders. Picking up their heavy burdens, they posted themselves to one gang or another and slid and slithered after them as progress was made.

The trouble with a headloader is that he cannot look down, but he compensates for this by wonderful balancing feats on one leg while his free foot explores carefully around for a sure foothold. If he slips he seldom loses his load but sits down on the steep slope and slithers on his backside until a tree stump brings him to rest with a jerk. He is nearly always lucky.

So in ones and twos, clutching branches, grabbing a timely held-out hand, slithering on their haunches, the men gradually lowered themselves down a slope which took the unencumbered Europeans all their time to negotiate. There could be no projection for it, but at last the column got down into a rocky chaung, full of miniature waterfalls, and the worst of the job was over. Looking up from the bottom, the hill seemed to rise up sheer and one felt rather pleased, but the Africans had already forgotten all about it and it never occurred to them that they had done anything out of the ordinary.

We got to the Taraw Chaung without further difficulty and found a pretty stream in front of us, so peaceful and quiet that it was impossible to imagine that the Japs could be anywhere near it. After a short rest "B" Company set off for the Pimples, our outposts were set, and we tucked ourselves away in a miniature gorge to await the arrival of the remainder of the battalion.

From where "B" Company started it appeared to be an easy matter to find the way but the bends of the Taraw Chaung turned out to be very deceptive and the company got temporarily lost. Moving with great difficulty along the hillside, more west than south-west, they suddenly came under fire near a small waterfall and had to break back on their tracks to find the real route. Meanwhile the remainder of the battalion came along, looking rather smug as they had found a guide who had brought them along without any of the mountaineering that we had had to do. They soon settled down into their new positions and the patrols which were then sent out quickly confirmed that both the obvious routes to Pyingyaung were watched and held.

By evening "B" Company had not got more than half way to the Pimples. The hill was precipitous enough, but the main trouble was that the bamboo grew so thickly that it had to be cut down nearly every step of the way. There were also numerous sharp spurs running down from the top which made it very difficult to keep direction.

One of the things which previous experience had taught us was that encounter battle seemed to result in more complications than the possible saving in time that immediate action might seem to warrant. It was therefore decided here to spend the night making plans and preparations rather than engage the enemy straight away. The enemy posts were not heavily manned, but their natural strength was great and there was no means of deploying a large force against them, so it was decided to make up two special forces, all led by Europeans, and to attack both posts simultaneously the next morning. These were to be found from "A" and "C" Companies.

As soon as it was light "B" Company continued its struggle up to the Pimples and the two fighting patrols set off to their tasks. On the southern approach to Pyingyaung "C" Company were opposed by some I.N.A., dug in astride the track, and they drove them out without difficulty when our mortar fire set the surrounding grass ablaze. But to the west it was found that both Japs and I.N.A. were dug right in to the rocky gorge by the waterfall and showed no intention of being evicted.

Less than an hour after they had left "A" Company were engaged in a spirited battle, and after a long time it seemed as if we might be held up. But they were too clever for the Japs. One of our sections managed to crawl up the hill and then round the right flank unobserved, where it lay up overlooking the track along which the Japs might withdraw. The mortar officer meanwhile got his weapons into action in spite of the steep slope and the many tall trees all round, and he then put his very first bomb right on the waterfall. When the remaining sections attacked, the Japs ran for it, and from there they ran straight into the ambush which was waiting for them further back.

It was a neat and successful piece of work in view of the strong position which the enemy held, and also because of the narrowness of the approach, caused by the river which ran very close to the track in this area. When they went on, they found that the enemy had prepared two more quite strong positions astride the track, but apparently they had not bargained on the hill being used as a line of approach and so made no effort to hold them.

It took "B" Company many hours to establish themselves on the Pimples, which had been called "X", "Y" and "Z", and a further considerable time to be sure that they really *were* on them. This involved climbing trees in all directions in order to get a view, and even then it was usually necessary to lop off the branches of other trees which otherwise obscured it. When I toiled up in their wake early the next morning I was not a bit surprised, for even on the track they had prepared it took an hour to reach the top, and the distance was hardly a mile. But it was a pity, for we had hoped that they would arrive in time to put out ambushes in rear of each of the posts which first opposed us.

It was now much too late to think of completing the operations in the one day. Battalion Headquarters had to be moved up the hill, "reccies" had to be made and a large dump of mortar bombs had to be formed since it was certain that the final attack in such rough country would require strong support. The plan was to attack the village from north and east simultaneously, while "B" Company in the centre could be placed in a position from which they could support either attack if it were necessary. The last hours of daylight were therefore spent in further preparations.

Point "Z", the westernmost pimple, was our O.P. It was described later by the Battery Commander as the best he had ever seen. From a convenient and most comfortable tree we could see the whole countryside laid out before us, as if we had been in an aeroplane. Straight in front lay the village, with a white footpath winding towards it among the mango trees; behind it the ground rose up to a bamboo-clothed spur, shaped like the roof of a house with its gable end falling sheer into the river; and behind again, with hardy trees and bushes clinging perilously to its sides, a great scarp of brown rock rose up from the south-east and closed in gradually to the river, where it overhung its banks for half a mile beyond the Gable. Far to the west we could see the Saingdin Chaung running on in its course to the Kalapanzin, just visible in the haze, with the grey-blue hills of the Mayu Range beyond. Only a picture could illustrate the mixture of peacefulness and wild beauty which lay before us, so while battalion headquarters was being set up, while the mortar officer got busy on the preparation of his dumps of destruction for the enemy below, we sat swaying in the branches of the O.P. and wondering at the beauty all around us.

Within an hour of dawn the mortars opened up behind us and began to search the whole area. They started on the little chaungs running down from the east, from which direction "C" Company was to attack, and then they switched first to the forward end of the village and then to its south-west corner. There was no sign of life and we did not hurry, carefully studying the pillars of smoke and dust with our glasses glued to our eyes as the concentrations shifted from one group of mango trees to another.

It was now April 1944 and we had been engaged on active operations since January. During that time we had fought three small but quite fierce battalion actions and for four days had also been attacked ourselves by nearly two Japanese battalions. In spite of that - up to this moment - I myself had not seen a single armed Jap. But now, fifty yards to the left of the last mortar burst, we suddenly noticed two tiny brown figures walking calmly across the open. They disappeared for a moment into the chaung which ran round behind the village, reappeared on a foot-path the other side, and then were lost to sight in the bamboo at the foot of the Gable Hill. Then others began to appear, and there was a feverish two or three minutes while the bombs fell all around them, but seemingly never on them. They too disappeared into the bamboo, walking no faster than the moment we first saw them.

It is astonishing the amount of explosive required to kill one man; and we could claim no victims here. But from the blood and equipment found later in the village it was evident that our searching fire had had some effect. We relayed what we had seen to the companies at the foot of the hill, and in a very short time the report came through that the village was clear.

It had thus been a very simple matter to take Pyingyaung, but our task was to clear the whole track which went on beyond it and it was only now that our difficulties began. The patrols we sent forward quickly reported that there was only one possible way over the Gable, and that this ran up a narrow gorge overlooked on both sides by enemy positions dug into the slope. By this time another day had sped by and as night closed in we could hear the explosions of grenades and bursts of rapid machine gunfire echoing below us. The patrols were trying each time to find a new way or to pin-point the enemy posts. All through the night the telephone kept ringing, and signal orderlies would creep out of the darkness once more to report "no luck".

The action next day was a typical example of the slow, slogging process of jungle warfare. Probably there were no more than fifty to sixty Japs and I.N.A. opposed to nearly our whole battalion, but it was quite possible that they would hold us up indefinitely unless overwhelming force was employed. There was no way round. A platoon which had been organized to get astride the enemy's line of withdrawal reported - after five hours - that it was still over five miles from its objective: and the last stages of its march were unfinitely the worst. There was no direct way open either. But *that* we had anticipated during the night - the Japs were masters in the selection of ground - and the whole of the Mortar Battery were to arrive in our positions well before midday. It had also been planned to use dive-bombers in the main task of blasting the enemy positions.

By midday, when the aircraft were due to arrive, the battery had just finished their ranging on the target and the bombers were already approaching from the south-west. The battery commander quickly gave an order and a single pillar of smoke appeared plumb in the centre of the target. For the next few minutes we watched the terrible scene, fascinated. As the smoke spiralled up into the air it was blotted out by the first bombs in a cloud of brown smoke and flying rocks. We cheered. The silver aircraft swooped down one after another and the hillside on which we stood shivered beneath us. It was a crescendo of sound, with a background of snarling engines like some unobtrusive yet necessary accompaniment. As the aircraft sped away, the battery opened up again to cover the time lag while the assaulting troops made their way towards the objective, and we watched delightedly as its bombs searched out every likely spot on the Gable.

After such a spectacle one might have expected that "D" Company would have had no difficulty in forcing their way to the top of the hill, but it was only now that the battle began in earnest. Very soon after the aircraft had gone, we watched the troops crossing the open area of the village and covering the leading platoon as it filed up the path into the bamboo and disappeared. But almost immediately after that the firing broke out.

The next hour was one of considerable tension. The firing was surprisingly intense and we could see the dust of many grenades rising up through the bamboo. If the enemy were still there, even if there were fewer of them, it might be necessary in such a place to repeat the whole process over again. There was no sign how the battle was going. No wounded nor runners carrying messages appeared on the track, and we had just to sit and watch with what patience we could muster, relieving the tension by directing the mortar fire slowly back towards our own troops as far as we dared.

But there were hopeful signs too. It was obvious that our own fire was carefully controlled, for there were moments of pandemonium and then increasing periods of complete silence. It seemed, each time, to us too that perhaps the firing was a little further up the gorge, and it turned out later that this was the case. Under Sgt. George, who was subsequently awarded the D.C.M., his platoon slowly drove the enemy from one position to another along the precipitous banks of the ravine, while our own mortar fire closed in on them from the opposite direction. As the sun sank lower in the sky we watched the remainder of "D" Company filing forward, halted interminably at the edge of the bamboo, and then disappearing in twos and threes among it. Then with dusk closing in the message at last came that the hill was clear.

We felt pleased with the result. It was a typical jungle battle. With a battalion, a mortar battery and eight dive bombers, we had only achieved our objective against less than a hundred Japs in four full days of strenuous effort.

CHAPTER IX

PRE-MONSOON

DURING the time that the 5th Gold Coast were fighting at Pyingyaung it was discovered that the waters of the Saingdin Chaung, west of the village, were brackish, so in spite of the fact that we had succeeded in opening up a direct way to the Kalapanzin, it was decided in the end to be impracticable.

But the battle was not without its uses, because it undoubtedly led the enemy to believe that a thrust was contemplated in that direction. In the meantime the greater part of the division had concentrated near Mazegyaung Khamwe, or "Point 77" as it was more generally known, and the airstrip at Pyhinla had ceased to be of any value. From point 77, after a period of rest, it was planned to move north and west through much more broken and hilly country which the Japs would probably never expect us to use.

The battalion had been promised a position in reserve as soon as its operations were over, and as we made our way back we were very pleased to learn that it involved the role of backstop at Dipa, for this meant that we should be on our own which was always popular.

It seemed most appropriate when we got there that the mail had come up, and the drink ration too, and the harbour the 2 i/c had prepared for us was shady, and had been comfortably furnished with a superior selection of bamboo chairs and tables. The very anticipation of comfort on operations, however, always seems to bring about an immediate move to somewhere less pleasant. It never failed with us. In this case we had barely started to unpack before a liaison officer - that harbinger of bad news - appeared to tell us that we were required at once at Point 77, and that only a company should be left behind at Dipa. The language greeting this news was pretty fiery, but we had learnt to expect this sort of thing by now.

Judging from the many comments made about this sort of thing during the war, it appears that a lot of people invariably put it down to bad organization. The soldier, however, learns from the most limited experience that while plans are the basis of operations, they can hardly ever remain the undeviating rule by which they must proceed. The enemy are fools if they allow it. It would be a miracle if the staff could forecast the future. He therefore accepts changes of plan with irritation but also with understanding, and he does not expect the general to come and see him and to tell him why the change has been necessary. It is much simpler and much pleasanter to put a little trust in the people up above, and to remember that they *have* to put it in you.

Our experience was that commanders are much more ready to listen to objections and to adjust their plans than is generally imagined, and that the views of subordinates were often pressed with considerable force. It is the time when no opportunity exists to object or discuss - and there are so many such times - that an order must be acted upon in the loyal assumption that it is completely right. On the other hand there are times when it would be madness to stick rigidly to an order, and it is only the natural soldier who senses when to discriminate between one and another.

The move of the whole battalion to Point 77 - less the one Company at Dipa - was a dangerous move, which might have met with a minor disaster. At best it secured the Division against the dangers of a surprise attack, but it could never arrest a determined thrust from either the south or east. South of the Saingdin Chaung, with a lateral line of communication which could easily be blocked for thirty-six hours, "B" Company was left in an area which was overlooked by high ground from all sides, and with an unfordable river in its rear. Over a thousand Japs had been reported a few miles to the south and it would have been a simple matter to seize the bridge at Pyhinla, block the narrow approaches from the other directions, and then to have dealt with the company at leisure.

The Japanese attacked on the same night that the Dipa position was occupied, but it was a half-hearted and unimaginative attack and they were driven off with considerable losses. No attempt was made to cut the L. of C., which might have involved us in costly counter attacks, and the effort was not repeated. We found it rather difficult to understand, but the probable answer was that it was at about this time (April '44) that the Japanese power in Burma had reached its zenith and was rapidly on the decline. In the Kalapanzin their attacks in the Taung Bazaar area, and against the passes across the Mayu range, had caused them crippling losses in proportion to the small forces engaged, and against us in the Kaladan the result had been much the same. Now their ambitious project near Imphal had drawn off the majority of their best troops and we found ourselves more than once opposed to engineer and reinforcement units. While like any Japanese they certainly attacked very bravely it was quite obvious to us, with our short experience, that their tactics were based more on theory than practice - the preliminary shouts and war cries, the L. M. G. fire to distract attention, and then that stealthy creeping forward from a different direction; the showers of grenades and the hail of inaccurate small arms fire. We were not to be caught out by that; actually we never had been, even when their methods were cunningly varied.

Our march across from the Kaladan had so far been completed ahead of schedule and Point 77, the General decided, was the place to rest the now tiring troops. For all HQs and for the administrative units it was, for we found it a most beautiful spot. But it was only comparatively so for some of the others.

Coming down from the north a broad, clear stream gurgled through the centre of our "box". There was a little wooded island in the middle of it, in autumn tints, and below it the water ran over a vast slab of rock or cut its way through in a maze of smooth and queerly shaped channels. It swirled in pot-holes and slid away into silent pools undercutting the rock, as one might find it in some imaginative and highly ornamented garden. To sit beside it in the evening sunlight listening to the shouts and laughter of bathers further down, or watching the constant stream of chattering headloaders carrying back the day's air supplies - that, and then to feel the security of ten thousand troops watchful on the hills all round was to know real restfulness.

Here the whole day long the atmosphere vibrated to the harmony of a new brand of grasshopper; nick-named the "knife-grinder" or the "saw-mill". He was rather an idle fellow, only beginning his operations long after the sun was up, but from then till dusk the noise he made was continuous and deafening. There was always a leader, who would start off with a noise rather like a hand siren, but then a hundred others would join in, working up to a crescendo, dying away like the notes of the "all clear", and finishing with a series of exhausted and rasping clicks. This was *not* restful, but patience and tolerance was shown on both sides. A lashing out by some exasperated officer only brought a moment's thoughtful silence and a puzzled "click-click". "Not musical", probably the grasshoppers remarked, sadly shaking their heads. And then it all began over again.

It was alright for the majority, but hardly for the subaltern. His patrols - day and night - still had to go on. There were the escorts to find for supplies to the out-lying companies, the track reconnaissances for future moves, and daily the changing ambushes to be set. It does not matter where the enemy are, and the Japs, even at this stage were not idle.

Among the hills opposite us to the west, the "Sierra Leones" had had several sharp clashes with brave but over-optimistic fighting patrols. We ourselves knew that there was another small party wandering, rather lost, in the jungle to the north-east, for it had made several attempts to break away at night but had bumped into outposts or ambushes every time.

There was an occasion when we had a most profitable action through a platoon commander being unable to carry out his orders. Late in the day this officer had suddenly been told to post his platoon on the south bank of the Saingdin Chaung. It had required some time for him to get his equipment together and by the time he reached the river it was pitch dark and too dangerous to make the crossing. He therefore decided to dig in for the night on the edge of the air-dropping site and forgot to tell anyone he had done so. And it was here that the unfortunate Japs, who had most carefully reconnoitred an unopposed way straight into Sierra Leone's Headquarters, ran right into them. Both parties were taken completely by surprise and the platoon commander was bayonetted over a cliff, to be followed almost immediately by one of his corporals with a Jap throttling in his hands. But the enemy were the most shaken, and ran for it, and in their hurry to get away forgot completely about both the ambushes they had so carefully avoided to begin with. Several of them were killed, others were badly cut about on the "panjies" which surrounded the positions, and the next morning one of them, very frightened, was discovered hiding in a barrel on the air strip.

The panji (pronounced pun-jee) was a form of obstacle which we had only recently learnt to use. We had never been able to carry wire, but we had quickly come to the conclusion that the panji was even more effective. The enemy could cut wire, but there was no answer to panjis except to pull everyone out of the ground. They were very quickly made by splitting a bamboo into three parts, about two to three feet long, sharpening the ends into a point and then sticking them at an acute angle into the ground. The Africans could erect a field of these, several yards wide, in a very short time. They were very difficult to see against the general background of green, and very tricky to walk through even if you knew they were there. We had learnt of them from the Japs, but while we invariably used them, they only did on very rare occasions.

The General was at his best during this period. If it was not exactly a holiday, he made it seem very like it. Everyone was getting very tired by then, and with tiredness often follows depression, but there was a galvanizing effect in his cheerful, confident figure as he strode around each day paying visits to every unit. The troops were a little afraid of him, but they admired him greatly. He was always known by them as "a proper general", which may have been rather a back-hander for other generals they knew but nevertheless was true. He was always neat and spotlessly clean; quick, alert and cheerful. The Africans always drew closer when he came a round rather than edged away. Everything he saw seemed interesting, and if there were difficulties he seemed to have a way of making you brush them away yourself.
"We'll have a swimming gala here," he said one day to the G.S.O.I. "Occupy that hill and it'll be quite all right." We weren't too sure, but there was no argument.
"If they come close enough, at least we'll know where they are."

So it came about that during one warm afternoon in the middle of the jungle there was a scene as carefree and cheerful as almost any other aquatic sports; but hidden in the hills on either side were bren gunners covering the water front and the gun crews at the battery site were standing ready to open fire at a moment's notice. The slippery pole was there and parachute cushions for pillow fights, and a tent of gaily coloured parachutes on the rocks by the water's edge for the General and his staff. The steep banks were black with laughing Africans, joking good naturedly among themselves over the lesser physical attributes of the "white Batouri". They have no highly developed sense of competition but love to sit and watch an organized spectacle and look forward for the chance to crow at the misfortunes of their fellow beings. It was a happy scene and a pleasant escape for a few hours from anything connected with warfare.

It was during the pause at point 77 that cholera broke out again within the division and several Africans died of it. This was a bit of a shock, because water discipline was generally very good and there was no village upstream which could provide a possible source of infection. But at least it served to show, even more strongly than the first outbreak that it is madness for anyone ever to take a chance with water in a tropical country. In this case it was thought to be fly-borne, and flies—however strict the suppression - are almost impossible to control completely when ten thousand men are bivouaced close together for more than three or four days.

The toll of sickness in this campaign, as in all others, particularly in Burma, was far greater than that extracted by the enemy. It was generally learnt in the Burma campaigns that training in hygiene and sanitation, and particularly in how to live comfortably in the jungle, was just as important as any other form of training. In fact one might describe these three things as the only big difference between jungle and any other form of warfare. It was also found that individual training in these matters was not enough: the thing had to be on a unit basis in the form of a routine. Thus you might work bare-chested throughout the day but there had to be a definite hour when anti-malaria clothing was put on, and mepacrine had to be issued in the form of a parade.

Here, because for many days there had been no suitable place for an air-strip, the field ambulance were filled with cases of typhus, the few who were recovering from cholera, and the usual cases of malaria and dysentry. Each day that went by where evacuation was impossible made the force less mobile, for stretcher cases had often to be lifted fifteen miles without reliefs for the stretcher bearers, who had to maintain the same speed as the marching troops. That they normally did, was due to the miraculous endurance of the African carrier. In actual fact there were numerous occasions when sick and wounded men were compelled to make their own way over this terrible country as best they could, and though few of them were much the worse for it, their patience and endurance should not be forgotten, and will always be remembered by those of us who witnessed it.

Curiously enough the Africans suffered very little from malaria, although the usual type in Burma is different from that generally met with in West Africa. It was the European who suffered continually: a day or two off colour; then perhaps a respite; then a visit to the Field Ambulance: a week or two of good health and then perhaps the same process repeated. The answer to it was the daily dose of mepacrine without fail, but when battles are being fought and patrols sent out with no certain time of return it is difficult always to apply the theory.

It was not absolutely certain that unfailing regularity with mepacrine would completely prevent malaria, and added precautions were the use of anti-malarial clothing and the application of mosquito cream to the hands and face. It can be imagined how contrary this was to all normal inclinations in a hot, sticky climate and therefore how high a standard of discipline and instruction was required. But it is quite possible that many cases of sickness, which were presumed to be due to the malaria parasite, were actually an unknown type of fever or simply the result of accumulated exhaustion.

There were certainly very many Europeans who lost a great deal in weight, whose appetite deserted them as the days went by and whose sense of humour died away. It was hardly possible to evacuate them when there were many more definite cases to be handled, and so it came about that we had to form a rest-platoon in Headquarters Company where they had some chance of recovery. This led to Africans being compelled to command platoons for the first time, and though they could neither read maps nor write messages, we soon realized that their ability was far higher than we had imagined. "There is nothing - with patience - that you cannot teach an African" was a truth that we began to realize at that time.

In some respects Point 77 resembled the position at Kaladan, for here again we were surrounded by hills and the possible exits could be blocked very easily by a small force of Japs. But from the moment we got there nothing was left to chance. All the time we were there, there were strong raiding parties operating at the maximum distance from the main force, and within this ring the Sappers reconnoitred the whole area and prepared no less than three routes by which we might move when the time came to do so.

There were few, if any, obstacles, which our force could not scramble through or over if the worst happened, but the main task of the Sappers was to ensure the smooth flow of our very long columns. This required the construction of large numbers of log or bamboo foot-bridges, of steps and staircases and the cutting away of steep banks. There was also a tremendous amount of sign-posting to be done - rather dismal work for highly trained engineers but of the utmost importance so far as we were concerned. As at Kaladan we got away without any opposition.

This was another march that many of us are not likely to forget. We set off at nearly midnight after forming up in a damp canyon, where forbidding slate grey rock frowned down on either side of us. Night marching is never pleasant: there is always the desire to lie down and go to sleep, and the longing for a smoke at every halt. Map distances seem to stretch themselves until you feel certain that the map must be wrong, and every check in the column seems more prolonged and irritating than ever it is by day.

This march was made infinitely worse by the fact that our path, practically the whole way, followed the beds of chaungs and led us back and forth, waist deep, from one bank to another. All through the night we ploughed and sloshed our way through water, turned into a sort of soup by the feet of the thousands in front of us. At many of the halts the men were unable to sit down because they found themselves between the vertical banks of a chaung, and at dawn, in the clammy mists, we found ourselves faced by a river which came up to some men's armpits, and which had to be crossed and then re-crossed within a matter of two hundred yards. It was by no means the hardest march we did, but in dragging our feet mainly through water for nearly ten hours it was certainly the most unpleasant.

The force rested for one day at Letpanywa while our rations were replenished by air, and then the march continued. A few miles to the west of it a ridge looks down into the tiny village of Taragu, far below, and beyond it we looked once again into the flat valley of the Kalapanzin in which our campaign was to draw to its close. Here while the main forces of the 15th Corps were thinning out in order to get back to suitable monsoon quarters, our task was to secure the left flank until the heavy rains had waterlogged the paddy fields and so made any large scale movement impossible.

The prospect hardly filled us with enthusiasm. The country here was very different to what we had been used to. It was dry and rather dirty, and there were queer, sharp little hills, rather reminding one of musty chocolates strewn haphazard about a table. They were only covered with low scrub and there was little evidence of the friendly bamboo to shade us from the sun or give us shelter from the rain. There were slimy pools and muddy streams, the grass was brown or blackened, and clouds of dust rose up at every step. We pictured ourselves soaked and miserable while the Powers-that-Be leisurely inspected the pitch, refusing again and again to reach the longed-for conclusion that rain had finally and irrevocably stopped play.

Nobody, we learnt there, should ever believe a word about the clockwork regularity of tropical weather, for it is impressive but untrue. When you are actually on the spot you will inevitably be told how unusual it is to be so late (or so early), so heavy or so light. "It's never been like this before". In our case everyone "who knew" - didn't; and the monsoon arrived, to the knowledgeable ones' surprise, most surprisingly later "than usual".

On the whole, though, the period we spent there was not unpleasant. The daily digging and the patrols - always the patrols - went on: positions were changed and re-occupied. There were gun busting expeditions and ambushes. It was a time of hide and seek.

The enemy were there, but it seemed that there was an air of the Gentleman's Agreement about it all. It was permissible to beat up a careless or over-bold patrol, and if we should secure a part of one feature the Japs might - to save face - attempt to drive us off another. There were random shots from the artillery on both sides and the small daily incidents of patrol warfare, but in general there was a feeling of live and let live on both sides; or so it seemed.

We found it a particularly valuable interlude in the troops' experience. Since leaving Kaladan they had noticeably gained confidence in their own ability, and slowly but surely learnt that it was no longer necessary for them to rely utterly on the guidance of Europeans. Here, day after day, they were sent off on quite lengthy patrols by themselves and moved confidently over wide stretches of open country, or among the abrupt and complicated little clusters of hills which characterised that area. They were liable to be shot up from any direction but felt by now that they were quite capable of dealing with a situation.

We were given a very good example of the value of a clear intention and definite orders at this time. South of our area, on a feature known as Long Ridge, there was a Jap outpost holding a pimple within a hundred yards of the 4th Battalion (Nigerian). They had attacked it continually, for the policy was to harry the Japs as much as possible, but the only approaches were steep and narrow spurs, the sort of position the Jap delights to hold. Well dug in, and with his automatics, as always, sited to the very best advantage, he had defied their efforts.

Until our battalion was ordered to relieve 4 N. R. there had been no urgent reason to evict the enemy. The Japs were not aggressive and apparently not in touch with their own artillery, and while they were undoubtedly suffering casualties, the Nigerians had not. There was no urgency in the orders given them, and so the position remained untaken. When it came to the take - over, however, the Brigadier took rather a different view of the situation.
"It wouldn't be right," he told the C. O. "for you to hand this over with the Japs still there."
"You yourselves are going out to rest. You will therefore capture the position before you go."

The relative position had not been altered as a result of these orders, but the Japs were immediately evicted because the intention for the first time was really definite.

When we inspected the enemy position an hour after the battle we were greatly impressed, and quite grateful that we had not been called upon to carry out the task. Every approach, we found, was a strenuous hill climb in itself, with little or no cover, and each was overlooked. It was true that the attackers had been given useful mortar support, but it was not at all an easy target for mortars to deal with because the spurs were so steep and narrow that most of the bombs fell harmlessly on either side. Mortars were seldom sufficient in such situations, so we felt it must have been a most plucky and determined attack to have induced the Japs to flee, as they did.

Long Ridge became a bit of a problem to us. It was very long and very narrow, and therefore not an easy place on which to site a definite position. As it ran not across our front but away from it, it was still more difficult. Our task was to keep the whole ridge clear if we could, but at least to ensure that the enemy did not gain its northern tip, which overlookd our L. of C. and the whole front over which eventually we would have to withdraw. It appeared that we were in for an easy time at first, since the japs disappeared from it after 4 N. R's. attack, but after a few days they came back and one of our routine patrols bumped into them further south.

For over a week we gave them a very poor time, but our luck was out. We ambushed their supply party but a stupid African, firing too soon, prevented that from being a real success. We successfully drove them off one pimple only for them to secure the next because a flank platoon failed to reach it first. We caught them bending-literally!-by night but failed because the excited Africans, instead of driving their bayonets into such a tempting target, fired instead-and missed. It was a pity, because the jap reacts automatically, correctly and like lightening to fire, but is very frightened indeed of an African charging with a bayonet. We also mortared them continuously for several hours on two consecutive days and received direct evidence of the considerable casualties we caused, but we failed altogether to achieve our object. It was another typical example of the campaign, in which it was impossible again and again to employ our full resources because of the nature of the ground. The answer is perhaps that it is militarily un-economic to attack such positions with infantry. If they can be avoided they should be contained or ignored, while of their capture is essential, the very maximum pounding by the R.A.F.-with no expense spared-is the only certain solution.

Occupied as we were in these small affairs, our days of waiting for the final withdrawal passed quickly by. The increasingly heavy rains were an unpleasant nuisance but they did not quench our spirits, and the slowly flooding paddy fields were almost unnoticed. One day the long awaited order came through, and the final plans were settled.

Curiously enough the tension of those last few hours, as afternoon drew on to dusk, and as in darkness the minutes dragged by to "Zero," was almost the greatest that we had experienced. There was a broad chaung to be put between us and the Japs and, had they got to know of our intentions, it would have been no easy matter to get the men away in the dark. But at last we stood watching the final patrols each slip away in the darkness on their final protective task, and the group of guides splashing their way quietly northwards to their various posts. The rain had stopped and the night was still. A little later it was Zero. The long, dark forms of platoons and companies loomed ghost-like in the moonlight: there was a pause for a few whispered words, the clink of a piece of metal, here and there a whispered curse and the last move had begun.

Like so many others, this was a watery march. We discovered that the paddy fields were nearly a foot deep and to march across them for nearly three miles in darkness seemed intermiable. But the last strain of contact had vanished and this made all the difference. As we reached the guide points and river crossings, or passed mysterious bodies of troops sitting silently by the road side, or the Sappers still working to the last, there were jokes and muffled laughter instead of silence or curses as before.

Next day we passed through Taung Bazaar garrison, pitying them at the thought of their sojourn there all through the monsoon. Two days later we were in our lorries on the Arakan Road. It was very hot and incredibly dusty and there was no comfort about it.

But, lorries!

Lorries after several hundred miles on foot were luxury under any conditions. The troops cheered and sang, and as we sped our way northwards, in a more sedate manner, we did the same.

CHAPTER X

REST, RECUPERATION AND RAIN

IT will be remembered that, while the main body of the 81st Division moved across to the Kalapanzin valley, a subsidiary force consisting of the 1st Battalion (Gambia) and a battalion of the Punjabis withdrew slowly northwards from the Pi Chaung, to cover the flank of the artillery and M. T. column which had to be evacuated along West African Way. The enemy pressed them closely with a strong force, thinking that the whole division was withdrawing in that direction. They drove them back slowly towards Frontier Hill which, in spite of very heavy casualties, they captured, and then they carried on their advance until they had taken Mowdok.

But by this time the monsoon had set in in earnest, and it was impossible for a large force to make much progress in such wild country, where most of the tracks were nearly six feet under water. There was therefore no very great threat to the Arakan Road from this direction, but it was a faint possibility and it had to be met. So it was that 4 N.R., who left us so jubilantly at Long Ridge, was almost immediately hurried off to the Mowdok area to be followed almost at once by the greater part of the 1st Battalion (Sierra Leone). Other parts of the 6th Brigade followed one after the other, and in the end practically the whole formation remained in contact with the Japs, although they had had more than six months strenuous campaigning behind them.

The remainder of the Division, concentrating at Chiringa, about 70 miles south of Chittagong, found that a rest period was a good deal less restful than they had imagined. The first thing we discovered was that we ourselves would have to build the greater part of our own camp, which was supposed to have been ready on our arrival. Most of the bamboo bushes were either half finished or not even started, and every inch of the side roads had to be latticed with logs if any transport was ever to use them. We had to puzzle out and dig a deep drainage system and practically every bit of carpentry had to be done by ourselves.

It was all done cheerfully enough, for the African is always happy when he is working hard, but we were not impressed by the zeal shown for our comfort by the L. of C. formations who should have dealt with it. It seemed to be a general experience in India that camps were never more than half finished by the time they came to be occupied.

The indignation which eventually found its way into the press with regard to welfare conditions in India was far from being without foundation but even after that it is doubtful if the real meaning of welfare was fully understood. To so many people the word implies canteens, wireless sets, books, cigarettes and tea; but these are really amenities, not welfare. It had a more subtle definition, I believe, that something which is connected with the supply of certain luxuries and amusements. It is more bound up with the attitude of the authorities, military and civil, than with the volume of commodities distributed.

There was an inescapable feeling in India that not the war, but the army was a nuisance. Whether or not it was *right* to feel that was another matter; but it was felt. Among the greater part of the Indian community it was impossible not to feel that we were an excellent medium for profit, but little else. There was a feeling that authority had partially given up the unequal struggle against piled-up inertia and indirect obstruction. In any case we were at war, after all, one felt it was being said; so the troops must be prepared to put up with things.

The railways were rather a typical example. There the rolling stock alloted for troops was the worst, and the oldest, that could be seen. The carriages practically never had lights, the conveniences were filthy, and if water supplies ran out it was an even chance that no more would be supplied. This was a civilian aspect of welfare: the movements personnel had their hands full enough in solving their problems in that general and invariable shortage of material.

That the higher staffs knew little or else did nothing about the more obvious causes of complaint was evident when electric light was promptly supplied immediately after Lord Munster's visit. If it could be supplied so quickly then, it is curious that it could not have been done some time before.

Canteens and leave hostels were not so much bad, as unimaginative. It was impossible in them to get away from the atmosphere of camp and barrack room: there were the same chamber-pot, tea cups or enamelled mugs, the dreary tea urns, always so dreadfully prominent, the squared oil-cloth; bare boards, tables G. S. and army posters. One felt that some had done his best, but someone with other and far more important jobs to do. There was a war on. It was quite true, but Welfare had a special application in such a country, where for so long the prospects of ever leaving it seemed so utterly distant. Everybody appreciated there must be difficulties, but they were not always clear how great they were. Careful and sympathetic explanation would have gone a long way, even if it did take up valuable time.

Then there were the Americans. If they required a building they agitated and got it. If they wished to deface a race - course with lorry parks and hutments, they were allowed to do so, but no British camp must inconvenience a civilian enterprise. The Americans had their little cinemas everywhere - not a canteen cleared for the occasion, but a cinema and nothing else. Their films were up - to - date - not old and discarded films, which the public no longer required. The whole of the Fourteenth Army had at a late date less that twenty projectors to cover the immense area over which it was spread, yet it seems inconceivable that an appeal to the British public would not have brought forward more than they could have used. It was known that we could not maintain the same standard as the Americans — in fact many did not wish to do so - but there did not seem to be much effort to lessen the gap.

It was the *known* effort which would have counted most. It would have been better to have announced the intention to increase pay or reduce postage rates, rather than to do so suddenly after months of silence, because then the concession would have been known to be voluntary instead of being thought of as the result of continued and increasing pressure. It must have taken a long time and great effort to work out the plan to decrease the length of service spent overseas, yet nobody knew about it until the plan was almost complete. Until it was announced, the troops naturally felt that they were perhaps doomed to many years abroad, and so they had nothing to look forward to to set against their hardships in India and Burma.

The Army in Burma *was* rather a Forgotten Army for a while. In the early days it was always short of equipment and often short of rations. The men were well aware of their many feats of patience and endurance, but also felt that the people at home were clearly not aware. This was perhaps the greatest mistake of all. It made them feel that the distance between them and their homes was almost immeasureable.

Nevertheless the difficulties which had to be contended with in India were certainly some excuse for this state of affairs. Whatever people may say in order that the best possible relations may be preserved, the people of India as a whole could not be said to be "in the war." Nobody would question the effort of the Indian Army, but that was not India. The immediate feeling of friendlessness was quite striking to one arriving in the country from an African colony. Except in so far as it affected their living conditions, the vast mass of the illiterate population seemed quite unaware of the war. Jobs were just jobs; and to be done with no more sense of urgency than they are ever done in the East. Let it also be freely admitted that there were also large numbers among the educated classes who cared nothing but to see the last of the English and all their works.

It is difficult to get very far while working in an atmosphere of thinly disguised hatred, and this was clearly present. Then there was inefficiency, waste and abuse. Seething as it was in the processes of a great change, India was hardly an ideal base for making war, and in such conditions it is not surprising that human problems were sometimes forgotten or set aside.

Life in Chiringa was primitive but not unpleasant. It will be remembered that the whole coastal area of the Arakan was fed by the one road and by the small quantities of coastal shipping which could make use of Cox's Bazaar. Soon after our return the whole problem became still more acute because the heavy monsoon rains proceeded to wash away two of the biggest bridges in the area. It made it quite an expedition even to get away on leave, but the supplies came through nevertheless. There were no amenities provided. Units had to find their own canteens, which actually were a great success, and there was an Ensa show and one or two cinema performances. It did not matter to us, for the Europeans were nearly all officers or N.C.O's, but the effect of such fare over a long period can be imagined among private soldiers who have neither the means nor the initiative to amuse themselves.

It was not the rain and the mud, we found, nor the boredom which went with the monsoon that worried us, but the fact that nearly all of us at once became subject to "prickly heat." This maddening rash, which looks like measles was the greatest trial we had to bear provided otherwise that we kept well and were fully occupied.

After a fortnight's absolute rest, the business of training began again. We had once more to build our own rifle ranges and to construct assault courses, to make our targets and aiming rests. The African N.C.O's had to be given a concentrated course of instruction, and all the lessons which we had discussed and learnt were due to be put into practice. During it all there were the leave parties to be fitted in.

We based our programme on a period of five to six months, but the time was of course, almost immediately cut down to half that figure, and in the shortest possible time, it seemed, we were preparing once more for the order to move again into battle.

In our first campaign, during which the amount of equipment we carried was twice reduced, we had come to think that we were existing on about the lightest scale it was possible to devise. It was only the thought that the reductions were a temporary measure that prevented us lapsing into the deepest gloom. Our absolute horror can therefore be imagined when we were told that not only would the scale not be restored, but that it was to be reduced by at least another twenty-five percent.

The idea seemed madness, especially as we should be operating for some time in the monsoon, but our virulent protests were of no avail: office boxes were cast aside, ammunition reserves were reduced and even personal kit cut down. When the division first started it had been resolved to travel light, but this was our third reduction since then. Yet we experienced so little trouble on our second venture that it is difficult to imagine what we could have been carrying when we started. Somehow we contrived to keep both clean and dry, and we certainly acquired a feeling of rich superiority on witnessing later the vast loads that other formations were apt to regard as their absolute minimum.

The period at Chiringa was brief enough, but no shorter than any of us wished. If there was another job to do, "let's get on with it," was the general feeling, and there was a feeling of relief when the day came to set off once more.

CHAPTER XI

DECEPTION

THE second campaign for the 81st Division began towards the end of September 1944. By that time the monsoon had slackened but it was by no means ended, and with but one groundsheet for our protection we did not view the prospect of another march over the hills with very much enthusiasm.

On this occasion there was to be no M.T. Apart from the fact that it might take two months to repair West African Way, there were few of us who did not consider transport a danger and a nuisance. Far better, we felt, to forego its minor advantages and to be free to disappear at will, appearing anywhere unexpectedly and fading away again without a trace. The Sappers thus were free to cut tracks by the shortest route to our destination, thereby saving a lot of time, but approaching periously near to cracking our muscles and breaking our spirit at the very start.

Normally the tracks we made would follow the chaungs as far as possible, only cutting over the hills where it was necessary to get from one valley to another. But as this time of the year it was not possible to follow the river beds, and from the very start we were faced with heartbreaking climbs, which we knew must continue until we got back on to the Kaladan. Because of the mud, it was insufficient merely to cut a path, for no headloader could have kept his feet in the circumstances, and so it was that the Sappers executed a feat which can hardly have a parallel in British military history.

For over seventy miles they constructed steps at every smallest gradient, footbridges over every myriad watercourse, hand-rails at very many places and stepping stones at every quagmire. We were too weary to count the steps up any hill, or down the other side, but there must be many steps in a "thousand-footer when the track must twist and turn interminably so as to follow the easiest, and often the only possible gradient. It was a magnificent piece of work, for the heights were in thousands all the way.

We found that while we hated the snails' pace uphill climbs, we preferred them if anything to going down, for when you have jarred your way down several hundred steps, none of them uniform, with falls of up to eighteen inches, it sets up a quivering of the thigh muscles which may go on for half an hour. It was a fact that often we looked down longingly, through a gap in the bamboo, to see how soon we would reach the valley below. There was no relief either climbing up or jarring our way down.

The frontier which we had crossed less than a year ago, breaking a twig for luck before we crossed it and then throwing it on the far side, was now held by the Japs who had dug themselves in there strongly during the rains. The old jeep track had been built over the only reasonable pass available, and though there were one or two subsidiary passes in the vicinity, they were also held. No doubt the Japs felt confident that they could hold us up for a long time, employing the very minimum of force, for the vigorous probing of the 6th Brigade, which had now begun, had shown no progress.

Looking at the map there seemed indeed very little prospect that a large force could be got across elsewhere. The ridge extended north and south for many miles and its eastern side, nearly everywhere, was vertical at the top: in those places where it was not vertical, it appeared that there was no reasonable approach from the west. Further north there were possibilities, though the country was very broken, but if we should succeed in crossing here it would mean that the Japs could turn to meet any attempt we made to move south, or be in a position to threaten us from either flank. The new divisional commander, Major-General Loftus-Tottetiham, was determined that it was we, not the Japs, who should call the tune, and so it was decided, in spite of the obstacle it presented, to get over Frontier Ridge, somehow, to the south.

The second campaign began therefore with the 6th Brigade concentrated around West African Way and probing vigorously at the pass, while 5th Brigade and Divisional Headquarters concentrated behind them in the area of Singpa.

Singpa was a few miles west of Frontier Ridge, and from it another ridge, parallel to it, ran southwards. Along this the 7th Battalion (Gold Coast) were ordered to cut their way, and from a base on it to send out their patrols to find a way east. From the base they selected it was only two miles, as the crow flies, to the frontier, but the nature of the task can be judged when it is shown that the main patrol had used up three days rations before they managed to reach their objective. It was not so much a matter of finding a way over, they found, as of even finding a way down from their base or then up again to the frontier. However the way was found, the ridge was reported clear, and the valley beyond showed no trace of enemy movement. At the end of the fifth day the hungry patrol got back, the Sappers at once were set to work constructing their innumerable steps, and in the shortest possible time 7 G.C.R. had crossed the frontier while the enemy continued to fight on in false security astride West African Way.

The next steps were comparatively simple. While 7 G.C.R. secured the valley beyond, 8 G.C.R. were quickly passed through them to secure the west bank of the Kaladan and the remainder of 5th Brigade followed more leisurely behind. At the same time the attacks by 6th Brigade were stepped up in their intensity and a very powerful air strike finally enabled them to dislodge the enemy from the pass. Within a few days the upper reaches of the Pi Chaung were secure and 8 G.C.R., sweeping north, failed by an hour or less to cut off a large force of Japs, who had only just begun to realise that things were not quite as they should be.

It was thus that what might have resulted in a long drawn out battle turned out to be a highly successful action with hardly a shot fired. Such mobility was only possible on our headload organization and because we could be supplied by air. It was a most heartening beginning for the campaign.

Before the campaign started we were given to understand that our role was to secure the upper reaches of the Kaladan, so as to prevent any wide turning movement by the Japs which may prejudice the operations against Akyab. The prospect of a comfortable period of static warfare after the previous hard campaign was not without its attraction, but of such stuff only soldiers' dreams are made. It would have been idle for anyone of experience to expect that to come true. Our operations had been far too quick and too successful for us to be permitted henceforth to stagnate in idleness among the hills in a purely negative role.

Almost at once we learnt that a further bite was contemplated - this time southwards towards Paletwa. The protection of the left flank of XV Corps could equally well be achieved from there, while if the enemy could be led to believe that our move was offensive, he might well be compelled to draw off more troops from the main front.

For this second phase there had to be a period of deception, for the main approaches to Paletwa ran through narrow defiles along the west bank of the river, and they would be very difficult to force.

With probably two battalions and possibly a brigade or more, the Japs - once they discerned our intentions - could dispose their forces effectively to deny all the likely lines of approach. For some time, therefore, the 81st Division was disposed on a very wide front. From Frontier Hill the 6th Brigade were moved rapidly down the Pi Chaung (parallel to and west of the Kaladan) where a strong Japanese force was blocking the approach to Bidoneyaungwa, the old route by which the right of the Division had broken through to the south in the previous campaign.

In the centre, on the west bank of the Kaladan, the main part of 5th Brigade were in contact with the enemy, while on the east bank the 8th Battalion (Gold Coast) and a part of the Reconnaissance Regiment were operating astride the old Jeep Track, which ran southwards to Thayeattebin. Since we had made a play of forcing the Jeep route across Frontier Ridge in our first manoeuvre, it was felt that the Japs might think we again intended to make use of transport, and so he was more likely to retain the greater part of his forces on the east bank of the river.

Accordingly 8 G. C. R. were given orders to maintain the greatest activity astride the road, probing this way and that as if we intended to discover the enemy dispositions in preparation for a major assault.

The deception worked. Every move of 8 G. C. R. was watched assiduously by the enemy, and, as the days went by, reports from "V. Force" kept coming in to show that they were moving reinforcements to that side of the river. It was also discovered that a Japanese General had established himself north east of Paletwa, so it looked as if this time they intended that there should be no mistake. But there was. After a short time the order was given that 8 G. C. R. should secretly be withdrawn to the west bank whereon the advance southwards, in the centre, was begun with the greatest possible speed.

In the period that most of these manoeuvres was taking place, the 5th Battalion (Gold Coast) were in position on high ground just east of the Pi Chaung at Sepeo, where their task was to guard the right flank and rear of 5th Brigade. Apart from routine patrolling and one or two special long distance patrols, there was nothing to do in this area and we had no contact with the enemy. We did, however, make our first contact with the American airmen, who came over daily in the Dakotas to drop us our supplies.

We had long become used to the way these aircraft skimmed the trees just over our heads, but one day one of them came so extremely low that we instinctively ducked as it went over.

A moment later the telephone rang. It was from A Company's O.P. "Hallo," it reported "Aircraft crashed. Bearing XYZ. Seems to be on fire." A second O.P. rang up to give another bearing, and the search parties and stretcher bearers were organized and rushed away.

It seemed most unlikely that anyone would be saved, for the aircraft had ran straight into the side of the hill, but in less than an hour the whole crew came in, very shaken but with no bones broken. They had jumped for it at just the right moment. We rigged them up with bamboo beds and produced blankets and parachutes for them to lie on. It was an event.

At that time we were under the impression that our rations were pretty good, but we could not help noticing that the Americans thought they were very, very bad. It was not rudeness: they just felt that we deserved something better, and promptly sent off a long message for specialities and beer. Unfortunately practically nothing turned up, and they ate very little for the first few days. Porridge was quite beyond them, and tea was no substitute for their beloved coffee. We were not hurt about it. In fact we felt with some satisfaction that we must be pretty tough if it were possible to enjoy something which others viewed with such obvious distaste. It delighted us when one of them asked how far it was to the nearest town.

After about a week the signal came through for them to go back and we sent them off with an African escort to a half way point on their journey. Three days later the Corporal confirmed our worst fears about their reactions to our hills.

"Massa", he said with a mixture of indignation and amazement. "Them men no fit march at all!"

"Why Corporal?" We asked. What had happened?

"Uh! Massa", the Corporal grinned "...... That big man, Sah. He march for ten minutes: then he halt for one hour! When I try help him, he lie for ground. He say "Go, go! Leff me, Corporal. I go die!" The Corporal chuckled. "They no savvy this march palaver at all!" It was no more than we had feared.

TEIMECYAUNG PYA.

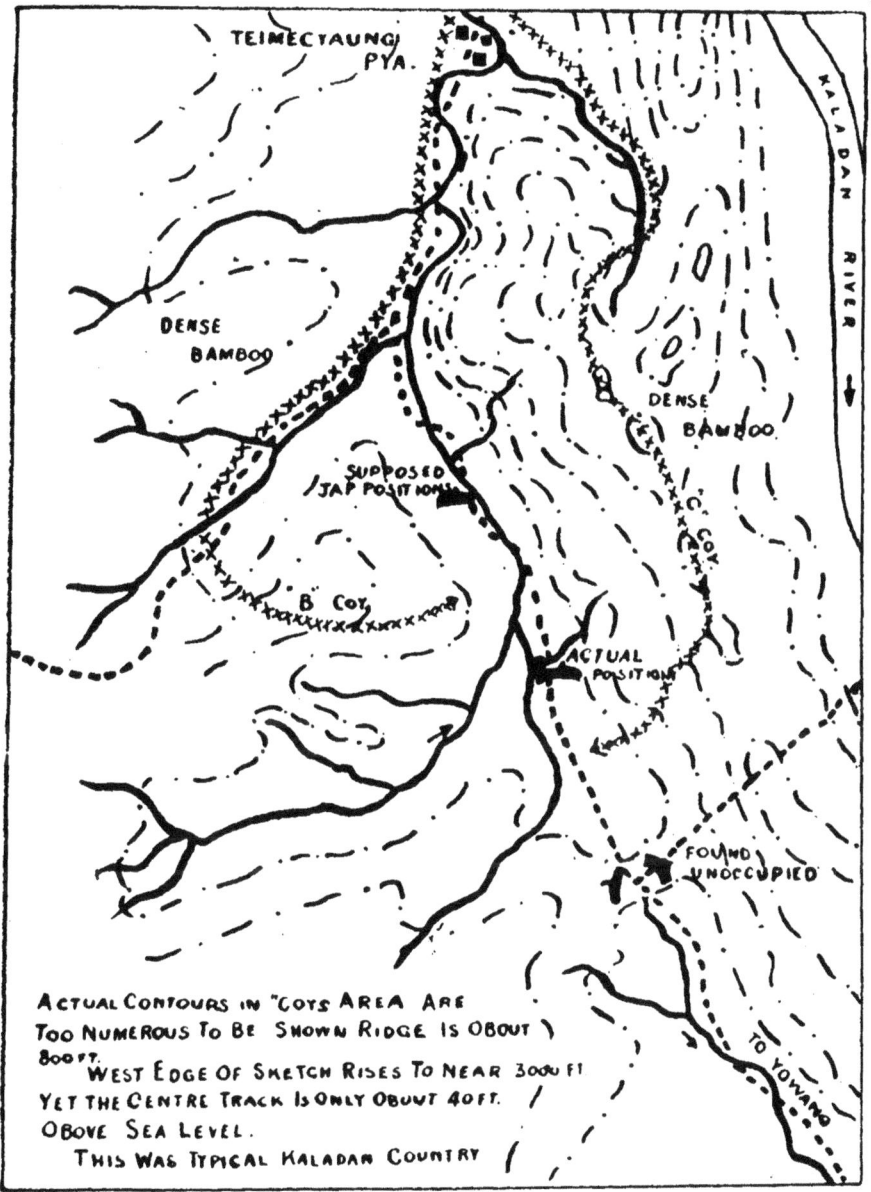

After a fortnight at Sepeo, orders came through for us to move on to the Kaladan, and the 6th Brigade took over the Pi Chaung with orders to clear it down to Bidoneyaungwa. We were sent to a new bivouac area on the banks of the river near Hnonbo, and it was in this area that we made our first contact with the Jap artillery which later was to give us a bit of trouble.

Within a few days the advance southwards began in earnest. While one company of 8 G.C.R. remained behind on the far side of the river to keep the Japs guessing, the remainder of the brigade was to move rather inland, to descend on Paletwa from west or south west. Patrols of the "Recce Regiment" moved in front, followed by 5 G.C.R., and along the almost vertical scarp, which divided our valley from the Pi Chaung, "D" Company was sent out to block progressively the three or four tracks which ran between them. It was unsatisfactory to be the leading battalion and at the same time to find a flank guard, but the answer came back that it was unavoidable.

V. Force had already discovered that there were enemy detachments astride the line of advance and very soon the "Recce" made contact with them. As usual, it was not a pleasant route, but narrow and twisting in dense jungle, with the inevitable steep sided and bamboo-clad slopes on either side. When we came up, the "Recce" patrols reported an ambush near a tiny village called Teimegyaung Pya and voiced the opinion that there was probably something a good deal stronger just behind it. They pointed it out to us and it all seemed quite likely, for there was a saddle in rear of it and it was common for the Jap to try to confuse by inviting attack on his outposts while maintaining his real strength in the rear.

It was clear in such confined spaces that anything but a wide flanking move would be slow and expensive, and so the process which we had at last learnt to apply was begun. Laboriously the mortar O.P. made its way right to the top of the hills to the left, while "C" Company passed through them and then along the top to block the enemy's rear. The instructions to the R.A.F. were prepared for the next day, while "B" Company made their slow and painful move to the assault from the opposite direction. It took over twenty-four hours and it would have been successful if the enemy had been where we thought they were. But it was a case of wishful-seeing: the "Recce" had pointed out the place they thought and after two hours with the binoculars we had imagined that our eyes had confirmed it. It was even possible that the mortar officer *had* seen movement in that particular place, but when the attack went in it fell upon thin air. What was worse was the fact that "C" Company, after a forty-eight hour struggle with cliff faces and narrow ledges, came out in a place two hundred yards on the near side of their objective. There, an unlucky clash with a small forage party 'blew the gaff' and the enemy in the main position made a hurried exit before "B" Company had a chance to block their escape.

It might be argued that no large scale deployment should have been made until our own patrols had confirmed the presence and exact position of the enemy's forward posts, but it was not done because we had found before that intense patrolling not only disclosed the size of our own force but often put the enemy wise to lines of approach which hitherto they had not considered. As it happened, a most laborious move was entirely wasted, but it might have resulted in the complete surrounding of the whole enemy force.

The last stage of these very disappointing manoeuvres threw a rather interesting light on the changed morale among the Japs over a very short period. As soon as the original objective was secured, a fighting patrol of "A" Company's was pushed forward along the sandy chaung towards the actual ambush that the Japs had laid. The enemy were still there at the time, and their position was quite a good one, but the Japs merely fired a few bursts and then fled when they saw our men charging in.

These, we knew, were our old enemies, the 55th Cavalry, and this was far from what we expected of them. It is curious, though perhaps understandable, that the after relief we experienced from so easy an operation there were several who expressed their disappointment at the falling off of their old opponents.

Just behind the ambush position we discovered the main Jap position sited on the saddle as we had half expected. It was undoubtedly about the strongest we had yet come across, carefully concealed, with every approach covered and with cunningly cleared fields of fire, so arranged that people could walk into them unexpectedly within fifteen yards of the enemy's automatics.

All this was abandoned, with hardly a shot fired, and a coolie who came in to us later described how the Japanese had danced for joy when the order came through, telling them that they would be withdrawn from the Arakan front.

After our fruitless labours we rested for a day in occupation of this unused position. As it was on the source of a small stream, it was damp as well as having that peculiar and unpleasant atmosphere that lingers on all old Japanese positions. Though they were nearly always amazingly neat and tidy, there always seemed to be an odour of sour sweat and something indefinably creepy about any place they left, and we were glad we were moving on.

The next morning "A" Company's progress appeared to be unusually slow and we hung about impatiently for the news that they had reached their first bound. This was a cross-tracks only a mile south, which it was important to secure because the country opened out there into a broad and much clearer valley.

It was necessary to place stops astride the cross-track because the Japs might well allow the leading troops to pass through to pounce upon the unsuspecting column following on. Going forward to them it was found that their lack of speed was harshly surprising, for the path, following the chaung led between very high banks, twisted and turned as if it could not decide which way to go. The African appears literally at times to scent trouble and Major Brooks, who was edging his men along behind the leading platoon, was insistent that they must be allowed to make their own speed. We had learnt on too many occasions that most European attempts to "get a b - move on" met either with disaster or at least with some remarkably lucky escape. "Let them go their own speed," he said "and it will be the Jap who is caught out first."

He was quite right, because there were several experienced Africans who could tell by the most minute indications if enemy were about. Footprints, broken twigs and displaced grass meant more to most of us, I believe, than we realized, but very much more to the Africans.

Well after midday, sure enough - a speed of less than a third of a mile per hour-the oppressive silence was suddenly broken by the sound of rapid rifle and L. M. G. fire, and quickly afterwards the news came through that the track junction had been secured. There was a Jap position in front, probably covering the chaung which was our line of advance.

"A" Company's action then was admirable. In a very short time their patrols were out to east, south and west. Their H. Q. was on top of a small hill to the right of the chaung, and from a huge tree half way up the forward slope it was possible to see the whole valley running southwards. The troops were in form. Along the track which ran off to the right they had very soon ascertained that the village nearby was empty, but there were several positions there, and two or three very surprised Japs were sent scurrying into the jungle. To the east, the track rose up to the line of hills overlooking the Kaladan river, and here an African corporal with only a few men acted very bravely when he charged up a very steep slope and dispersed an ambush, which was in a very good position. The patrolling forward had to be very much more carefully done, since the dense jungle and the elephant grass along the sides of the chaung gave no indication at all as to where the enemy might be.

The mortar officer was building a platform in the tree as we surveyed the ground in front. Looking down on it, it seemed a possibility, though a dangerous one, that the battalion could be slipped right past the enemy positions which, if we had had four companies, could have been completely sealed off, but the remainder of the brigade were far behind and it was one job to clear away opposition, not to fasten it down. We were there to secure the Ru Chaung which

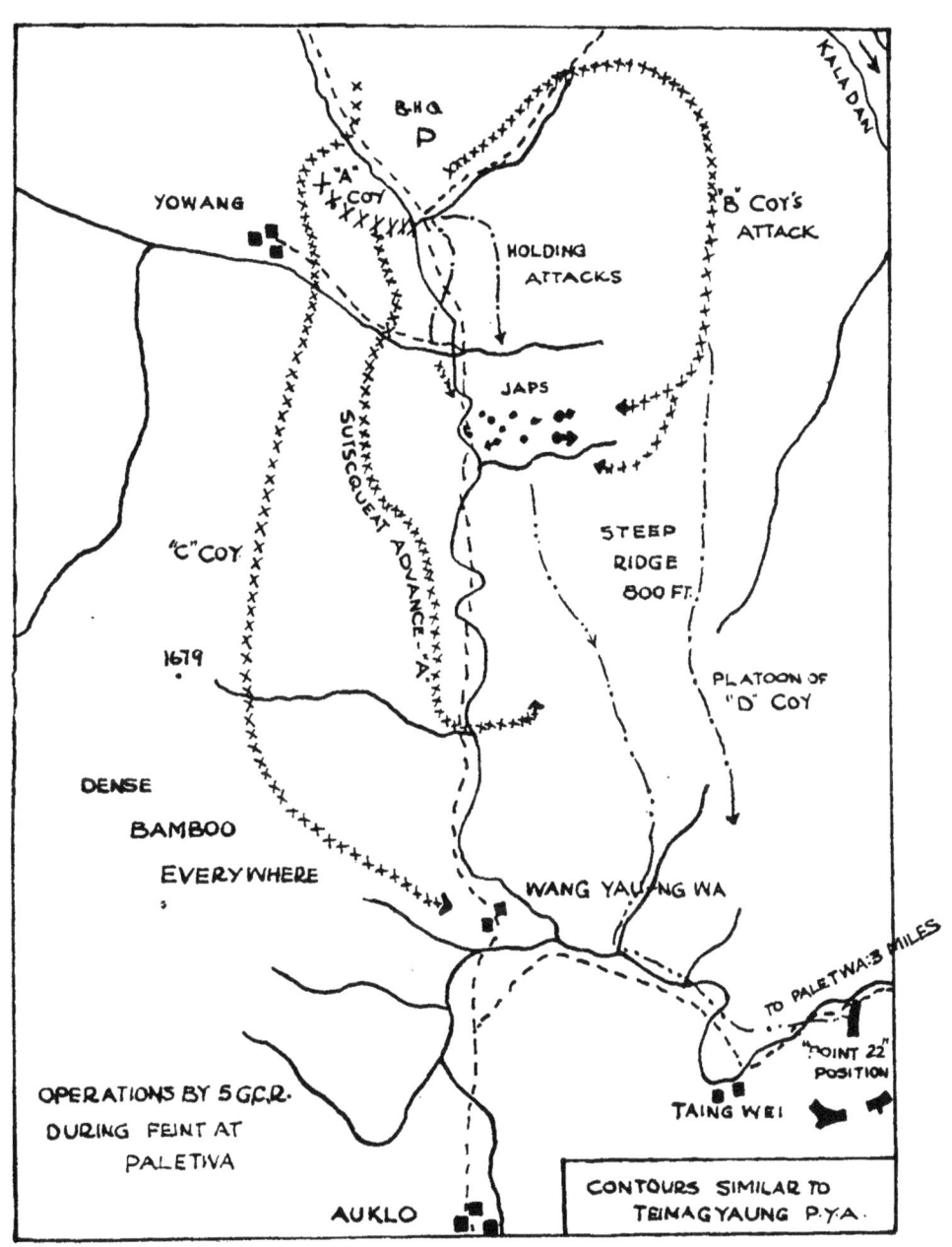

ran across our front a mile ahead, where the Brigade would be in a position to attack Paletwa. The battalion was therefore closed up on "A" Company and plans were laid for a new attack on the following day.

We were now well supplied with excellent air photographs well in advance of operations, and from a study of them with the ground it seemed that we might be able, not only to secure our final objective but to cut it off and clean up the enemy in the process. The chief difficulty was the absence of "D" Company, still on the flank guard, which meant that if we employed all the other three companies we might still have insufficient men and have nothing in reserve to maintain our base. A message from Brigade had just informed us that they would rejoin us shortly, but it seemed certain that after their scrambles along the top of the scarp to the west, and the long march to catch up with us, they would be in no fit state to indulge in vigorous action.

Without counting on their aid, it seemed that the ridge to the east offered the best chance of success, since it was so steep on our side that the Japs were unlikely to expect attack from that direction. We could by-pass another company to the west of secure the Ru Chaung, while "A" Company remained in the centre to hold the base.

After making this brief outline plan, and after only a mile-long advance, the night closed in, and our activities died away.

Early the next morning our patrols began again and the sustained bursts of medium machine guns showed that the Japs strongly disapproved our activities. We had been mortaring them at dawn, and it soon appeared that it had been quite successful, for a patrol came back to say that they had found the bomb bursts right in the target area.

The patrol was rightly rather pleased with itself since it had wormed its way right in to the enemy position, and discovered, not without a shock, that a gun firing behind them was Japanese and not one of our own. Fortunately the enemy were not at all sure what was going on and they opened up wildly with most of their automatics, with the result that the patrol's description of the whole position turned out to be quite outstandingly accurate. We were able to work on this and the final plan was decided.

It appeared that the enemy had only a small post on the Wang Chaung, and that their main position was on a spur running down from the main ridge, with a subsidiary post on a knoll behind. Both the latter looked down on and covered the post on the chaung, and also the ground to the west, which was flat and without much suitable cover.

After mortaring and an air strike, it was therefore decided that "B" Company would attack the position from left flank and rear by way of the ridge, while a platoon of "A" and the Defence Platoon engaged it from in front. In the meantime "C" Company would by-pass the Japs by the hills to the west, in order to secure the crossing of the Ru Chaung at Wangyaungwa (See sketch). When "D" Company arrived, they would secure "B" Company's L. of C. and cut off any Japs trying to make their way round Hill "X" to the Kaladan. Had they been there in the first place they could have secured the whole of the ridge, as well as Hill "Y" in rear of the Jap position, but arriving piece-meal as they did - and very tired - it was not possible to use more than one of their platoons until the operation was practically over.

After the company commander had made an intensive study of the air photographs, it seemed that the ridge approach would be quite feasible, and "B" Company set off before midday with orders to attack after the air-strike next morning. But within little more than an hour, the old story began to unfold. The telephone, as the line reeled out behind "B" Company, rang and rang again :
"The going's almost vertical here. Sorry, very slow progress".
"Held up. We're having to cut footholds".
"Sorry; haven't found a way down yet", called the Company Commander.
"If this continues I suggest the strike is delayed by at least half an hour."
Later in the afternoon, after a long silence, there was another call.
"How's it going now?" we enquired.

"Better!" They were down, at any rate - by the use of ropes and rifle slings. "Can you drop us a round of smoke, though?" asked the Company Commander. "We can't see a yard now."

All the time, meanwhile, as we sat in battalion H.Q. listening to the reports coming in, the mortars searched and plastered the whole area of the Japanese position, and repeated calls for refills of ammunition were sent back to Brigade. To the west, at intervals of an hour or more, "C" Company rang up to report their similarly slow progress to Wangyaungwa. The ground was the only trouble. They had come across an extensive enemy position on the hillside, but it had been abandoned, and there was no sign or opposition. In their post in front the Japs lay silent and utterly invisible from our O.P's.

At about 0900 hours the next morning the Hurricanes came in, dropped their bombs and then, one following the other, raked the target area with cannon fire. Then as they hummed away our own mortars again took up the tune while "B" Company edged forward for the attack. There was a short interval and then the firing broke out to the left, sending the echoes racing among the surrounding hills.

It was soon evident by the sound of the fire that the Japs had not suffered much, either as a result of the mortaring or on account of the air attack, and after a short interval the Company Commander rang up to confirm this. The only feasible approaches he said were all completely covered by medium machine guns, and it appeared that the air-strike had been too far to the right, where the enemy had abandoned the part of their position on the banks of the chaung. He could try again, he said, but the position really required further softening up. The attack was therefore called off. Another air-strike was asked for, and the mortars began their task again.

When this was done it was decided to infiltrate "A" Company past the Jap position, just west of the chaung, to secure Hill "Y" in the hope of cutting off the Japs when they eventually decided to withdraw. It was a reasonable move now that we knew the limited strength of the enemy, and in view of the fact that most of "D" Company had now caught us up. But a great mistake was made in withdrawing "B" Company from their positions in close contact with the enemy, or at least in not arranging that regular fighting patrols from other sub - units were not sent forward to keep them engaged. We had become so accustomed to the Japs doing nothing except by night, that the possibility of an earlier withdrawal was not considered. If such an assumption had been correct, then the move of "A" Company would have achieved its object.

Very unfortunately, "A" Company's move was almost as slow as "B's" and "D's". In their case it was not the ground which hindered them but the extraordinarily thick elephant grass, which they had to cut through nearly all the way and which, unlike bamboo, tends to spring back somehow into place, even after it has been cut. In addition, it appeared that our own mortar bombs fell so close to them that they had to make a much wider detour than had been calculated. It was therefore only well after dark that they reached and managed to secure the lower slopes of Hill "Y" and, as a result, failed to discover the L. of C. to the east of it, that the Japs had been using, until dawn broke.

The enemy had slipped past them - probably at the very time they were occupying Hill "Y". Next morning the second air - strike took place and when the attack followed, the position was found to be clear. The line of the Ru Chaung was also found unoccupied and we had secured it before noon.

Although we had secured our objective in reasonable time in that type of country, it had been an action of lost opportunities, which clearly demonstrated the need for a fresh appreciation of the situation at much more frequent intervals. When it was disclosed, for example, that there were no enemy on the right flank the need, no longer, to retain 'A" Company as a firm base might have been realised. The importance given to Hill "X" instead of to Point 22, which covered the direct route to Paletwa, was also a mistake. And the fact that the enemy were not kept pinned to their position after the first attack, was perhaps the worst fault of all.

There was also the element of bad luck in the proceedings, though it cannot be denied that by more careful planning it could possibly have been avoided. Evidently the Japs were seen by both "A" and "D" Companies when "A" Company was nearing Hill "Y", but each company mistook them for their own troops. Then it also came out - much later - that in "B" Company's original attack one of their platoons had actually reached a position which was feasible for assault, but were ordered off by the Company Commander because the mortaring was about to begin again. Since he could only see the situation from his own very limited view point, he had not thought it possible, when he made his report, that the third platoon could make more progress than the other two. It was unfortunate, but such situations were fairly common in our jungle battles and could only have been avoided if all the platoons had been provided with wireless communication. There was no time to call the mortaring off, since he himself was then a long way from the phone, and so a golden opportunity was lost.

Appendix B.

ON BEING SHOT UP ON PATROL

By Capt. A. W. Gauld.

ON the 22 November 1944 the battalion was occupying a position astride the Pi Chaung south of Ridaung. Reports indicated that the enemy were withdrawing south in the hilly country on both sides of the river. Two patrols from "D" Company, strength one section each, and led by African N.C.Os were detailed to reconnoitre two tracks which branched apart about one and a half miles south of the entrance to the Mizawa Chaung; one leading down the bank of the Pi Chaung to Letpanbyi, and the other going south-east over the hills to an unnamed village. When the patrols returned, it was obvious that they had not carried out the job fully, probably because they had done very little map-reading. Accordingly I was detailed to take two more sections on the same task on the following day, going in to the Letpanbyi with one and putting the other on the correct path over the hills.

Setting off at 0600 hours, and having sent off the other section at about 0730 hours, we were proceeding across the Pi Chaung when the leading scout drew attention to fairy recent Jap footprints leading both ways in the sand. One of the previous day's abortive patrols had reported seeing four Japs at this point, and said that they had run back on sighting our men. I had been sceptical about this report at the time, but it now seemed more likely. I therefore gave orders to move with even greater care, and we continued along one bank of the chaung.

After a little while, I came to the conclusion that the scouts were being far too cautious and urged them to get on, at the same time moving up behind Sergeant Musa Wangara who was third in the file.

By 0845 hours we were still moving steadily down the track. It led in and out of some fairly tall elephant grass, broken by quite long stretches of loose sand offering no cover at all. The Pi Chaung was between 100 - 120 yards wide at this point.

I was crossing one of these open patches, about fifteen yards long, when I felt a light tap on my shoulder. At the same moment three machine guns opened up from the opposite bank, and some rifles too. I was at least eight yards from cover and realized that it would be impossible to gain it in a single bound, so I took a leap forward into the loose sand and lay flat. My orderly did likewise behind me and shouted to the next man behind to copy him. The man behind him tried to regain the cover he had just left, but he was knocked over by a bullet through the shoulder. He was able to walk back later, however.

The African sergeant and the second scout, in front of me, momentarily lost their nerve and doubled back, the sergeant getting a bullet through the jaw which, luckily, did not prove very serious. While the leading scout who was almost in cover, dived into it and disappeared out of sight.

Meanwhile the three of us in the sand were not enjoying ourselves; as I dived to the ground my hat was blown off. My lighter skin was easily seen, and accordingly I was treated to at least one full magazine from across the river. It seemed to me incredible that anyone could score a complete wash-out at such short range, though there were a couple of near misses through my trouser legs. The other two men were untouched. However it was obvious that this sort of thing could not go on indefinitely, and I was just wondering what was the best course - or rather if any course existed - when I heard a voice which carried clearly across the chaung calling in English "Stop ! Stop ! - Stop firing !"

Why this happened, puzzled me for a long time afterwards. The only feasible reason must have been that the Jap officer believed that one or all of our motionless figures was wounded, and that he hoped to take us alive. Whatever it was, I was devoutly thankful and with a headlong dive reached the cover of a small crack in the hillside. My orderly did the same, but evidently the Jap fire control was not too good, and a sniper who was still firing hit him in the ankle. It would have taken a good deal more than that to have prevented him escaping from that ambush.

That was the end of the action. I wormed my way up through the dense bamboo, potted at by granade dischargers and gathered the others in. It was more than we could expect in being alive.

The moral is that it is extremely unwise to tell African scouts to 'get a move on' when they want to move cautiously. They sensed trouble and were always right. If they had been given more time, they would probably all have spotted the ambush.

The enemy's choice of position was as usual excellent. If their marksmanship were a little better, there would be many of us not living to tell the tale.

CHAPTER XII

DEVELOPMENT OF A THREAT

THE threat to Paletwa must by this time have become obvious to the Japanese, but the true intention on either side probably still remained uncertain one to the other.

During the period that 5 G.C.R. was forcing its way down the Wang Chaung to the area of Anklo and point 22, 8 G.C.R. less one company had crossed the Kaladan from the east to west and rejoined the Division. At the same time the Reconnaissance Regiment had completed a magnificent march along the whole length of the perilous ridge on which "D" Company had performed its blank task, and then had cut eastwards over equally broken country to the banks of the Kaladan, south of Paletwa. There they had an exciting time for several days, hiding away in the hills by day and shooting up the Japanese rivercraft by night.

The position, therefore, as the Japs probably saw it, was that there was still a battalion on the east bank of the river, a Brigade on the Pi Chaung and the majority of a Brigade on the Ru Chaung, directly threatening Paletwa. Quite probably they could only be certain that battalions were operating in each of these sectors, and so there was always the additional possibility that another force might by—pass them still further to the east. Their limited forces were thus stretched beyond reasonable control.

From our own point of view it must have been difficult to decide what exactly the enemy proposed to do. Up to now all his moves had been negative. In the Pi Chaung he had very strong positions and obviously intended to hold them, but this action against 5th Brigade north of Anklo seemed mysteriously indecisive. On the east bank of the Kaladan, also, his reaction to the movements of 8 G.C.R. had been entirely negative, yet there were continuous reports from V. Force and other local inhabitants that the enemy were concentrating considerable stores and large number of men to the north of Paletwa. The Japanese General's Headquarters was still known to be there, and it therefore seemed most likely that they would attempt to hold the place, or at least try to keep us involved there as long as possible. He may have been relying upon about 2,000 men to do this, which would appear hopelessly inadequate, but the Jap knows his ability to make the best use of difficult ground. A characteristic of his, though, of which he was not probably aware, was his pig—headed determination to deny anything at which his opponents might appear to aim, quite regardless of its importance.

While 6th Brigade continued to operate on the Pi Chaung, a new box was formed covering the Ru Chaung and Anklo. There was but one track to Paletwa in this area, which ran up the cliffs near Point 22 and then parallel to the river into the town. The positions occupied by 5 G.C.R. covered the south and south-east perimeter of the box, and it was within less than an hour of our arrival that one of our patrols discovered that the path up the cliff was held.

It was practically certain that the Japs would contest this defile but, since we required an exact pin-point of the position from an airphotograph, it was decided to send the Intelligence Officer with a small party to confirm it the next morning. The subsequent action was a typical instance of the difficulties and strain of jungle warfare against an enemy like the Japanese.

The I. O. and his party set off almost before it was light. His intention was to reach a point on the hills opposite Point 22, where he could first identify the position on the air—photo and afterwards maintain it under observation. There was no difficulty in getting there and, with the help of the patrol leader of the previous day, the enemy post was pointed out to him.

At a range of only three hundred yards, he then proceeded with two of his section to keep the post under continuous observation with field glasses for nearly six hours. During the whole of that time not a thing moved; nothing was heard, and not a branch nor a blade of grass appeared to be displaced. Nothing! But just at the end of that period his orderly whispered that he had seen something. The point was carefully described and the whole party kept it in view for still another hour. Nothing!

At this the I. O. decided that the place *must* be investigated more closely. The little party slid backwards out of its O.P. and after nearly two hours of crawling, listening, and crawling again they had reached the very point which the African had described.

It was at this moment - at a range of about twenty yards - that the Jap machine gun opened fire. The I. O. very badly wounded, somehow managed to stagger away by himself, but a Corpral was killed and two of the other men injured. Their own L. M. G. was left lying in full view. Luckily the remaining Africans did not loose their heads but, on the contrary, acted very bravely. Completely overlooked as they were, and still under furious fire, they first dragged the two wounded men out of danger and then retrieved the L. M. G. There remained only a rifle and that was brought in, though a man was killed in doing it.

The I. O. was brought in, and the section came back, quite frightened and certainly rather depressed by their losses. It made one marvel for the hundredth time that these men could show such loyalty with yet such un-material grounds on which to base it. In serveral similar cases, I feel sure, it was only merely blind obedience which actuated them. They had by themselves overcome the blind reaction to fear which is in all of us, and they had learnt a pride in doing those things which it was right for a soldier to do. But there was also a staunchness and a readiness for sacrifice which, to those of us who knew the limits of their mentality, was difficult to fathom. It created an obligation on us to serve them in their turn which I hope will not be forgotten.

Another air-strip was constructed at Anklo, so that the sick and the wounded might be flown out, and it was in the interval that this went on that the scope of the campaign was extended again.

The ease with which we had moved south and the situation in which the Japs were now placed - split into small packets over a wide area - made it obvious that there was little to prevent us changing to the offensive if we wished. The attention of by far the greatest part of the enemy forces in Burma by now was focussed in their effort to halt our offensive in the direction of Mandalay, and the information which for some time had been coming in from all over the Arakan showed that their role there was purely defensive. The whole outlook of the Japanese had changed. They had lost the initiative. The new plan was therefore to make an advance similar to the last campaign, but in a slower tempo, taking care never to overreach ourselves at any time.

The temptation in this type of country was to operate on the broadest possible front. It produced much more spectacular results. But it also placed a greater strain on the supply situation and it laid small forces open to the danger of heavy counter attack. It was dangerous in our case without a third brigade, which could be kept in reserve, and the Corps Commander ruled against it. Orders were, therefore, issued that the 6th Brigade should rejoin us at Anklo, and no advance was to be made in future without "one foot on the ground."

This move of the 6th Brigade produced a fine instance of the wonderful work which was being done by strectcher - bearers and heavy load carriers all the way through the operations. After the actions in the Pi Chaung there were some twenty serious stretcher case to be carried over the ten mile trek to Anklo. The ground was appalling. In the two miles to Laidem village it rose to twelve hundred feet; in the next one and a half miles, it twice fell four hundred feet and twice rose over five hundred; then it fell once again only to rise over eight hundred feet in half a mile.

It was here that the column reached the top of the great scarp along which the Reconnaissance Regiment had made their way to the south of Paletwa. It was dark when the stretcher parties arrived and before them lay a rock - face, slanting at an angle of forty - five degrees, dimly lighted by bamboo flares to help the men across. There were, of course, no handholds, but across the bare rock the leading troops had dug out a series of rough and ready footholds, little bigger than a man's hand. The Medical Officer who related the incident stated unashamedly that on seeing the obstacle he had discarded his sten gun and equipment, handed them to his orderly, and crawled across with a prayer on his lips.

It seemed unbelievable that in such circumstances - after such a march - the stretcher bearers with their unwieldy loads on their heads, in such a light, and only able to feel with their toes for each foothold, could have accomplished the passage at all. Yet the twenty wounded men were brought across without a single incident, and then down two thousand, five hundred feet to the safety of the air - strip.

In the Advanced Dressing Station for the next week, where it was my misfortune to be, there was certainly neither peace nor quiet. Soon after their arrival, 6th Brigade had taken over the task of blasting the Japs out of Point 22, and at short intervals, day and night, we jumped in our beds as one more series of salvos from the mortars roared forth only fifty yards away from us. Each day the Hurricanes and Spitfires rent the sky as they plunged down to rake the position with bombs and cannon, but still each dawn and dusk we heard the familiar rapid fire of the Jap machine guns as they gallantly announced to our fighting patrols that they still remained.

It had been obvious from the start that there was no possibility of a successful frontal attack on the position, and while 5. G. C. R. were still at Anklo their patrols had discovered a way through the hills to their flank and rear. But that was as far as anyone had got so far, for as usual it was found that the Japs held knife-edge positions, perfectly concealed and covered. It seemed as if they might never be driven out, but as time wore on the mortaring and air attacks began to take effect. Finally, after a day during which the Spitfires had straffed them from dawn to dusk, the commanding officer of the Sierra Leone Regiment himself led the evening assault and took the position.

These constant attacks near Point 22 apparently stenghtened the enemy's conviction that the divisional objective was Paletwa and the line of the Kaladan. At any rate, he had held on to it most determinedly and the information still coming in was of strong forces in the neighbourhood and also east of the river. In actual fact, the advance had continued far to the south and westwards with the object of securing the old Dakota-strip at Kyringi, where for the first time it would be possible to fly re-inforcements in large numbers and evacuate the sick.

The twists and turns that were made during this march were apparently quite incomprehensible to the Japs, for though we made occasional contact with their standing patrols, they were never able to assemble a strong enough force to oppose our moves.

Their mystification was perhaps understandable. What had we done? Our first move is made at full speed to the Kaladan, where a force is thrown across. Surely a bridge-head? Next we make for Paletwa, threaten it from the North, west and south, but do not take it. The 6th Brigade is transferred from the Pi Chaung to the outskirts of the town. We hammer at Point 22 for a week or more but, once captured, we lose interest. Instead 5th Brigade has already thrust due south; suddenly they appear again on the Pi Chaung, leave it again, veer back on to the their original course near Sanmeywa only to reappear on the Pi Chaung at Kyringi And during the whole of their move they had cut backwards and forwards over the formidable, trackless hills, when easy going tracks were everywhere to be found.

Such apparent aimlessness, and the speed at which these move were made, worked admirably. Apart from small patrols, the major portion of the enemy forces were still concentrated opposite 6th Brigade at the time the leading troops reached Kyringi. The Jap plans to stem any possible advance south were so far behind that at Sanmyaywa almost due east of Kyringi, the leading elements of 5 G.C.R. killed an Artillery officer who was still planning defence lines which were already far behind our leadind troops.

That the enemy were surprised in this instance was pardonable, but it was interesting to note that throughout both our campaigns the Japs failed to appreciate the factor which made them possible; that is the full length air fields, without which we could receive no useful reinforcements, or evacuate the large numbers of partially sick or lightly wounded. It is doubtful if they could ever have succeeded in preventing our securing without interference, some area where a moth-strip could be constructed but they never seemed to realize this was not enough for us. If we used Moths, it was considered good going if we managed to fly out fifty casualties in a day, but it was not feasible to fly in the same number of reinforcements, with their equipment, at the same rate. Therefore at certain intervals we were bound to require a sufficiently large area in which to build a full sized airfield.

If they had attempted to deny such areas, our difficulties might have been considerably increased, yet not only did they never try, but they also allowed us to use them for days on end without interference, The Jap tactics against us - I feel sure - were based on those he used on the main Arakan front, where, because the British forces were based on road communications, it was possible for him to hold up a large formation for weeks on end because the position he held eliminated the usefulness of a road until they were taken. On the Kaladan he attempted to apply the same tactics in respect of jungle tracks, quite forgetting that our air-borne supply system made no track essential.

Another possibility is that he appreciated that nothing could stop us bringing in reinforcements on the smaller air-strips if we really needed them, but failed to appreciate the importance we placed on the well-being of our sick and wounded. Since his own sick were of no importance whatever to him, should the safety of his force be at stake, he may well have credited the same feeling to us. The actual problem that ours at times presented might have opened his eyes to our requirements.

There was only one incidence of importance in the whole of the move from Anklo to Kyringi, and this was when a part of the main body of 7 G.C.R. was ambushed and suffered severe casualties only a little south of Anklo itself. Prior to the move, the advanced guard company had secured a village some way to the south without meeting any opposition on the way. The next company, moving the following morning, evidently assumed that the way was still clear, and the ambush was the result. The battalion was held up for some time dealing with the opposition and in the meantime 5 G.C.R. were ordered to by-pass it and secure Kyringi.

The incident is related simply because this was the only time in both campaigns that the Japs seized the opportunity to attack a column behind its foremost troops, and also to show how necessary protective detachments were in every part of a marching column.

At Kyringi little time was wasted. The "Loop" was quickly fortified and the airfield put into working order. At the same time 6th Brigade left Paletwa and followed by forced marches, but instead of branching west towards Kyringi they pushed southwards, after reaching Sanmyaywa, to the area of Kwangyaung. The main point of interest was that the Division had now been joined by an Indian Mountain Battery which slowed down the column considerably and provided quite a problem in the matter of harbouring. In many of the worst stretches, special paths had to be constructed before the mules could get over the hills, and it was even said that the Africans had to carry them in some places, though the Battery denied that this was true.

Once again speed was the watchword, and while 6th Brigade's wounded were being transferred westwards to the air-field, they themselves sped due east to Orama to secure the crossing of the Kaladan.

CHAPTER XIII

COUNTER-ATTACK AT TINMA

THE crossing of the Kaladan at Orama was as much a surprise to most of the 81st Division as it was to the enemy. It had been made known at Paletwa that Kyringi was to be secured, and the holding of a line between there and the river was known to be a reasonable possibility, but it was not till these objectives were reached that it was known we intended to take the last biggest bite out of the cherry - the capture of Myohaung.

Myohaung, the ancient capital of Arakan, is now but a dusty native village, somewhat larger that most of the others in the area, with only a hospital and a few administrative buildings to lend it added importance. There are still many pagodas, but none of its ancient glories remain. Militarily the town was of great importance, though, because it controlled the motor road which ran through it from Minbya, twenty miles south, to Kyauktaw. Its capture would, therefore, eliminate any further real threat to the Kaladan valley, but it would also lay open all the undefensible flat country which lay beyond, between Lemro and the Kaladan. This area lay athwart the landward communications to Akyab, which, since its sea lines were now cut, would be rendered untenable if we took it.

To the Jap's way of thinking, after the capture of Point 22, our next move should have been the occupation of Paletwa. Instead of that, our move southwards was so fast that they may not have been sure where we were for sometime. Certainly they had forces opposite Orama which could have made a crossing for us a slow and costly business if they had realized our intentions, but 6th Brigade's sudden appearance on the east bank was evidently such a surprise that these dispersed in confusion.

A little north of Orama, on our own side of the river, a patrol of the 4th Nigerian Regiment stumbled, in fact, on a peaceful Japanese pay parade for the local I.N.A. Quite unaware of our presence in the area, they were sitting about the village without having taken any precautions, and their surprise was comical. The patrol came back with broad grins on their faces, carrying sackloads of newly printed currency, and for several days afterwards there were odd parties of Japanese who came walking into our possitions, obviously quite unaware that things were not as they should be.

The enemy made no effort to counter-attack the river crossing but disappeared in small parties to the south. Within two days the 6th Brigade had secured a wide bridgehead around Tinma on the other side and the remainder of the Division closed in on it.

Since 5 G.C.R. had led the way to Kyringi, we had expected to remain there for a few days, resting, but it was not possible, and half the battalion were ordered to go to Orama to take over the west bank when 6th Brigade were clear. It was an easy march and we settled into a comfortable harbour with little work to do. But none of us liked it. In the first place we were scheduled to cross on a Friday, and in the second place, from experience in the first campaign, we had grown very suspicious of all river crossings. Curiously enough our suspicions, were confirmed, because it was at Tinma that we experienced the fiercest engagement in which we had yet taken part.

North of a line between Orama and Kyringi, the mountains rise and fall in a tumbled mass right down to the edge of every stream and river, but from this point southwards the paddy lands open out in ever widening areas, more pronounced on the west of the Kaladan but also in a long, wide belt running down the east bank to Myohaung. There are only isolated patches of rice field at Orama, shut in by the hills, and thick woods line the river bank, but at Tinma on the opposite bank there are considerable open stretches, one of which, about three miles inland, it was proposed to use as a Dakota strip.

The village of Tinma lies open on the river bank, but five hundred yards to the east of it a long ridge runs southwards, inclining inwards to join the river. Beyond it is a long strip of paddy, and other ridges beyond again, until the hills rise up once more to divide between the Kaladan and the Yau Chaung. Then there are unbroken hills to the wider Ru Chaung and finally to the Lemro.

Three miles to the south of Tinma the ridge falls down to Khataw and from here the stretch of paddy land grows slowly wider, until at Thazeattebin it is some ten miles across with only a few isolated hills and ridges to break the monotony. It is from Thazeattebin that the mortor road runs straight to Myohaung.

5 G.C.R.'s task was to secure about a mile of the north end of the ridge at Tinma and to deny the approaches between it and the river. In the meantime, until the arrival of the remainder of 5th Brigade, there was the Sierra Leone battalion to guard the northern approaches and other elements of 6th Brigade on the next ridge to the east. It was an easy enough task, but throughout the day the greater part of Divisional Headquarters had been using the crossing only it was only just before dark that the last company of 5 G.C.R. got across. Thus there had been little time for concealment, and it was in any case a strong possibility that all movement had been observed from the south end of the ridge.

That night we experienced the first concentrated piece of shelling in the two campaigns so far. At 2000 hours a deep boom disturbed our sleep and we lay listening to the sort of musical swish that a shell makes when passing overhead. The first salvoes were so far over us that we calculated, with some selfish satisfaction, that the bracket would fall on the centre of the village. Instead of that the first correction fell in the village and the second into the middle of our own headquarters. Then the rate of fire quickened and we cowered and prayed as shell after shell fell in the same area with its ear-splitting crash. For endless minutes it seemed as if each swelling, vicious buzz must seek out one's own foxhole, and we listened to the jangle of flying cooking pots and to the shrieks of a wounded man almost with relief to know that one of them, at least, had missed our mark. Then the gun suddenly switched and we breathed again.

Some thirty shells had landed within a small radius inside our headquarters, but it was a relief and an interesting lesson to find that but one man was killed and only three wounded. The Africans were not in the least shaken, but from that moment onwards they revealed themselves as even more efficient diggers than we already imagined them. On reaching harbour their foxholes and weapons pits took precedence over food, rest or conversation, and no instruction was required. Light head - cover over every trench became the necessity of the hour and several lives were subsequently saved from direct hits on account of it.

The next day 5 G.C.R's position were re-adjusted. A platoon of "B" Company had to remain on the west bank of the river, since elements of the division would still be crossing for the next three days, but the remainder of the battalion was either on or in the vicinity of the ridge.

About a mile below Tinma, the track running south along the river bank turned sharply on to the top of the ridge, where it ran along it to Khataw, and it was in this area that "A" Company was established, holding two pimples which covered the approach from the south. "D" Company held the lower slopes of the ridge on the other side, covering the wide strip of paddy which separated it from the next ridge to the east, and "B" and "C" Companies were in reserve behind, and overlooking the village of Tinma. Tucked into the cover of the trees and bamboo close by were the Field Ambulance and Brigade H.Q., and Divisional Headquarters lay only a little further to the rear on the western slope.

The enemy attacked on the following night, but by that time our strength on the ridge had been considerably reduced. It had been decided to send out a part of the Battery in an attempt to "beat up" the Japanese artillery, and "D" Company had been sent in support of it. Another two platoons were also sent on fighting patrol. Two platoons were therefore taken from "C" Company to cover "A" Company's left, and a part of the Field Company to support their right. The equivalent of only a company was left in reserve between Brigade and Divisional H.Q.

Not long after dark the Japs began their attack with heavy and accurate artillery fire, and followed it up with 3 inch mortars and with their loud and unpleasant "knee mortars." Then their infantry attacked.

"A" Company had put out a small standing patrol a short way forward along the ridge, but it could do little more than give warning of the assault, and was quickly over-run. The Japs appeared very suddenly and were able to shake out on either side of the section post, so although the gun team killed several of them they were in no position to remain; nor were they required to do so. An African can move very fast through thick bush, but the section had hardly got back to their company position to give warning before the Japs made their first charge at the leading platoon. They were met by a furious burst of fire and a hail of "36" grenades, and the charge wavered and eventually broke. Then the battle began in earnest.

At this part of the ridge the approach had narrowed to about the width of a medium sized room in any modern house, and the three platoons of "A" Company were therefore disposed one behind the other on a series of pimples themselves not bigger than a tennis court. It was not therefore possible for the Japs to outflank them, because the slopes would have been too steep for a charge and also because we could roll grenades down on them from above. There would be little to stop them by-passing the posts, particularly low down where the Field Company was in an unenviable position but luckily once he goes for a thing the Jap carries on till he succeeds or fails. Up, therefore came his machine guns to support his attacks, while his mortars plastered the positions behind, and his infantry rushed, fell back, and rushed again. Finding these tactics failed, they crawed forward and dug themselves in under their own machine gun fire, and heedless of the hail of grenades that were thrown at them. Then they would organize another charge and failing, dig themselves in again, always a little bit closer to our weapon pits.

The expenditure of ammunition was terrific. It *had* to be if such determined assaults were to be driven off, and there were many casualties on our own side incurred in the efforts to crawl forward with further supplies. On this narrow ridge the battle swayed backwards and forwards for nearly seven hours in the darkness, amidst "Banzai's" from the Japanese and counter yells of derision from the Africans, who were in their element. At one stage Jap and African were actually firing at each other at less than five yards range, and one African worried by the fire of a wounded Jap nearby, crawled out of his foxhole and finished him with his matchet.

As night wore on the casualties in the leading platoon began to mount, and with dogged determination several of the Japs reached and occupied some of our own trenches. The position was serious. It was not feasible to counter attack through such a narrow position, and there was a strong possibility that the Brens might jam under the strain of such sustained firing. Late in the night, therefore, the leading platoon was suddenly withdrawn during a lull in the battle. At the same time our mortars, which had been keeping up continuous fire on the enemy's rear areas, decreased their range to assist the withdrawal.

Knowing their enemy, the second platoon were fully expecting immediate attack, but the Japs had by then had enough and instead their firing slowly died down and they gave up. They continued to occupy the post they had taken from "A" Company for some hours, but vigorous counter patrolling gave them no rest and in the end they withdrew further and further along the ridge until contact was broken.

The troops had excelled themselves. As the ground lay, they could be given none of that flanking fire which normally is the real strength of a defensive position, but with rifle, grenade and automatic they had fought the battle out themselves at a few yards range. It was estimated afterwards that the enemy had used the greater part of two companies is their efforts to wipe out our forward platoon. Individual acts of bravery that night earned the company no less than one D.C.M. and five M.Ms. The details are shown elsewhere and they were well earned.

The case of a Bren-gunner from the standing patrol was particularly pleasing. When his section came back, this man stayed behind, and during the earlier stages of the battle dodged about, firing his gun into the assaulting Japanese from varying positions on the flank. Next morning he was found by his gun, alive but unconscious from lack of blood, with all his ammunition expended.

Our own mortars had been largely responsible for the eventual break-up of the attack, for it was found that their fire had done considerable damage in what must have been the Japanese reserve areas. Forty-five bodies were counted the next day, and since the Japs are normally very careful to remove every one they could, it is probable that the total casualties killed were as many as eighty or ninety or perhaps fifty percent of the force engaged.

From Tinma onwards, the Japanese artillery harassed our positions on every night they were in touch with us, and often during the day. It was on the same night that "A" Company was attacked, that the Japanese attacked our Indian Mountain Battery and succeeded in entering their gun positions and damaging one of the guns. From the observations of a sepoy, who had remained in hiding up a tree, it appeared that, once they held the position, the Japs evidently felt their task was done, there and then sitting down to eat their rice under the trees. A counter-attack, however, was put in by "D" Company and the guns were quickly recaptured.

Our 3.7 Howitzers, it proved, were practically useless for the task in hand. They were far outranged by the Japanese 75 mm and 150 mm guns used against us, and were seldom able to support us. But the Japanese gunners — a point which has been observed on other fronts— were quite evidently better trained in battle craft than our own. Whereas our batteries often appeared to make a hopelessly vulnerable target, the Japs almost invariably dug their guns right into the hillsides on a forward slope, only running them out to fire them. Nothing therefore but a direct hit on a gun, or right into the mouth of each little cave, could silence them. They never fired from the same area twice, or even remained in the same place for much more than an hour or two, and their mules, carriers or limbers were obviously moved during firing to some perfectly safe place. Nothing was too much trouble, and their technical efficiency appeared to be good: the rapidity of their fire was sometimes bewildering.

It was as depressing to our gunners as to ourselves to feel that we could do nothing to reply to the enemy bombardments, yet it was also a disadvantage that we were bound to accept. If we had had heavier guns we should have become tied to the flat ground parallel to the Kaladan, which was the very ground on which the Japanese were basing their defence of Myohaung. As things were we were free; and so there was only a pause near Tinma, while the Division collected itself for another rapid movement, once more into the friendly hills which would lend us cover practically the whole way to Myohaung.

The plan for the next stage was simple enough. If we were sometimes over optimistic about the number of casualties we caused, the enemy were possible even worse offenders. More than once in the first campaign they had imagined us defeated and broken as a result of their attacks, and there was reason to believe now that once again they were of the same opinion. They knew that we were still maintaining a small force at Kyringi, which may have led them to believe that we did not intend to carry through our thrust, and they may have thought that their artillery fire had caused considerable execution. At any rate, it was intended that they should think of us at Tinma as a force licking its wounds, and patrols were even sent back as far as Kaladan village to spread the news of an impending withdrawal.

There was, of course, no such intention, but while 5th Brigade remained for a time at Tinma, 6th Brigade made their way rapidly over the ridges to the east and thence down into the Yan Chaung. This follows for some twenty miles due south and then breaks out westward into the plain south of Thayettabin, so that an undetected move to the elbow might enable us to cut off the Jap forces to the north, waiting there for 5th Brigade's withdrawal. Thereafter it was expected that the 82nd West African Division would arrive from the direction of Htizwe and the Jap defeat should have been made complete.

This plan began to work effectively. From Tinma East, two miles inland, the 6th Brigade slipped away unnoticed into the hills while the Japs were kept occupied by constant patrolling from 5th Brigade. Then the latter slowly began to thin out until, a few days before Christmas, the whole area by the river was evacuated. The Japs were taken in. Suddenly finding the birds had flown, they sped northwards on the heels of the beaten enemy, only to find, some twenty miles up the river, that their adversaries had given them the slip again.

Appendix C

XMAS PARTY - 1944

By Lieut. Rother 5 G.C.R.

ON Xmas Day the battalion was holding a ridge some ten miles north-west of Myohaung, preparatory to the reduction of that town which was one of the main Jap Arakan bases. "Div" H.Q. was to move forward that day and in order to secure the next base, it had to secure a track which we knew from previous reconnaissance was being used by the enemy.

During the early hours of the morning I was ordered to ambush this track to cover the "Div" move. I was not to withdraw unless recalled or relieved. The ambush force I took consisted of two bren guns and the riflemen of one section. Two brens were taken in order to ambush the track from both directions. Every man was armed with three hand grenades which, as events proved, came in very useful. While on the subjects of grenades it is interesting to note that through both campaigns I endeavoured to make all my A.O.Rs grenade-conscious. So keen had they become of them that before any show they always clamoured for them. It was seldom that my platoon went into action with less than two grenades per man, and they helped us out of several tight corners.

Shortly before dawn I moved forward with my ambush to 'recce' the site. I did not have to go very far before I discovered one of those rare but beautiful positions that the infantryman dreams about. The track was covered from two directions by the bren gunners. The area covered along the track was ideal. It was chosen so that the enemy had to approach over a small rise, where the track bent slightly, and so he would not be able to spot us until he was ten yards away. But we ourselves could see him coming along.

I took up my position at a convenient spot between the two brens. The riflemen were disposed for flank protection and to guard the rear. There was plenty of cover in nice thick jungle into which the men crawled, clearing themselves small but useful fields of fire. The African corporal, who enjoyed this sort of thing, pleaded to man the forward gun post. Once that was done there was nothing for it but to wait for the blighters to come along! The time was about 0800 hours.

By about 1100 hours I was almost dosing at my post, the inactivity was beginning to get rather unbearable, and I was thinking the Jap would never come. Suddenly the corporals bren went off in a furious long burst that only Africans fire, and several grenades were thrown. I rushed forward to see what had happened and there, not five yards away, lay the bodies of three Japs and among them an officer. The two Jap privates died almost immediately; the officer though severely wounded, lived for about two hours. My corporal told me that a patrol of about five had approached and the last two had turned tail and run for it.

There was nothing to be done for the officer, and I was glad, for more than once I had seen for myself the cruelties and indignities they had inflicted on our own killed and wounded, too unpleasant to describe.

We went out to look at our kill. It was most satisfactory. For such a small show, the booty was considerable: a sword (my second), a pistol, binoculars; a very well made fountain pen and a rather intricate - looking gun sight which had not been seen before. Obviously they were a party of gunners, out to set up an O.P. There was a mass of other articles, but most important of them all was the Officer's haversack. It contained plans of the enemy dispositions in the area, maps marked with gun sites, and the tracks and rivers they were using as their L. of C.

We were quite elated by our success and without altering our dispositions, now sat down to wait, hoping for more to come along. There were no alternative positions anywhere nearly as good and the ambush had been so successful that I decided not to change it. The bodies were left lying where they fell as I knew that the Jap makes every attempt to recover his dead.

However, nothing happened till the late afternoon. My company commander had sent down the rest of my platoon for added protection, and I began to recce dispositions for them. But while doing this my carelessness struck me: the two Japs who got away would certainly bring reinforcements; very likely the present seeming lack of activity was a pointer in this direction. I looked round; we were overlooked by high ground on three sides, our rear could be cut off; my main force was in a very narrow dry chaung approaching the ambush; we could be attacked from almost every direction.

But in the meantime B.H.Q. had apparently come to the conclusion that the morning's party had been a highly successful one. The position was now to be held as a firm base, and a platoon from another company came down to relieve me. My company commander arrived to supervise the hand-over. "Look around," I said to him. "There isn't a single spot here where you can ambush the track and still make a firm base". So he had a 'duba' and agreed. Perhaps something could be found further along the track. A bren was sent forward to cover the recce and my company commander and I went forward too. While we were looking the covering bren opened fire and started to withdraw. We saw quite a number of Japs coming towards us, so we too hastily withdrew to the ambush.

'Duba' - 'look'

Now the party started. Japs seemed to be everywhere. We had a strong force; the fire power of two platoons was something to be reckoned with, although we were hemmed in by high ground all around. I rushed back to cover the rear. This was the danger spot. All the brens were being fired from the hip and the hills were literally sprayed with fire; it was almost a curtain that we put down. In the midst of all this the men from the rear covering party started to fall back—the Japs were behind us too.

The chaung we were in was narrow and winding. I went to have a look. Suddenly going round a bend I came face to face with a party of enemy less than fifteen yards away. I could not tell how many and withdrew round the corner from which I had come. The Japs must have been as surprised at the encounter as I was, for they did not come on. It gave me the chance to lob over a couple of grenades, and two A.O.Rs with me did the same. Groans were the result.

We had a cautious peep round the bend; two of them had fallen. The rest were haring back along the chaung. A corporal and his men gave chase, but they could not catch them. However our rear was now clear.

I now put a section in position to ensure that we would not be cut off again, and then went back to see what was happening at the ambush. But the fire had died down by now and another six Japs lay where the first lot had fallen. Apparently the ammunition we had let fly had been too fierce fro them and they were withdrawing.

My company commander decided that now it was really useless to hold the position. "Div" would have passed through. Our job was done, and so we retired to the battalion area.

Net result — ten enemy bodies. There must have been some wounded, but it was impossible to tell, and there was quite a bit of really useful information. Own casualties — one wounded, and a fearful expenditure of ammunition (6000 rounds of bren, about half as much from the riflemen, and last but not least, 63 hand grenades!) The latter, I think, carried the day.

Altogether it was quite a successful Christmas, though there were moments when we were not too happy.

The next day the battalion pushed on towards Myohaung.

CHAPTER XIV

FINAL OBJECTIVE, MYOHAUNG

THE Japanese forces at the time of this final operation of 81st Division were estimated to be about 500 in the area of Kyringi, and about 2,000 in the area south of Tinma. They were also supported by about 30 guns, mostly of 75 mm and 105 mm calibre. Against this we could oppose about 6,000 fighting troops, but only supported by mortar batteries and the one Indian mountain battery, which was far outranged by the enemy artillery. It seemed a heavy enough preponderance in our favour, but the easily defensible nature of the country has to be remembered, and particularly the fact that unless units were to be broken up into a series of disconnected fighting patrols, they could seldom deploy more than about a quarter of their strength at any one time. The question of supply and of the evacuation of wounded always mitigated against this, so that there was always a certain ponderousness when any large scale objective had to be attacked.

6th Brigade cut their way over the 2,000 ft. ridge, which separated them from the Yau Chaung, without incident, and the advance then continued rapidly down the valley until they reached Thandada, a village five to six miles south-east of Thazeattebin. Here the 1st Gambias completly surprised a two-section Japanese patrol and quickly captured the position. They then rapidly secured the area of Sin-o, a mile or two to the south, while 1st Sierra Leone seized Pt. 887 to the west, where once again a strong party of Japs were taken unawares and eighteen of them killed. It was here that a message was captured confirming the heavy casualties caused them when they attacked us at Tinma.

There were several small but fiercely contested engagements before the area was finally secured, so that the gaff was blown and the enemy hurriedly withdrew their forces from the north west. It was the case now that either they were too quick or the division was too slow, but at any rate they were to succeed in blocking our advance before it could begin again.

By the time that 6th Brigade had begun to secure the Yau Chaung where it bent westwards at Naleik, our own brigade were hot on its heels.

From Tinma, 5th Gold Coast Regiment had concentrated near Raka, where from a round hill which had been used as a Japanese O.P., the whole country could be seen stretched for miles around it. It was a magnificent and lovely view: south of Thazeattebin and the lower Kaladan, winding blue through the faded yellow paddy plain; west to dark Pagoda Hill, where the tide of battle had turned against us in the first campaign; north up the valley, with the mountains closing in and the jagged peaks of the Kantretaung above Paletwa clear against a cloudless blue sky; and lastly east - to the steep, mysterious ridge, showing no sign of the thousands who had already struggled over it, and which we were to tackle the next day.

As usual the Sappers had cleared the track and cut steps up and down the mountain into the valley beyond. It was just one more of a hundred similar climbs which now meant nothing to us, but it was too much for the mules of the Mountain Battery and we had to send out parties to manhandle them up the first and steepest part of the track.

Following in the footsteps of 6th Brigade, the battalion made its way over the ridge without incident and hurried after them into the valley of the Yau Chaung. In three marches we had reached Barje, just north of Thandada and the long period of our rapid movement came to an end.

By Christmas Day it was clear that the 82nd Division would not be able to join hands with us in time. It was also clear that the main Japanese forces would be able to get away unmolested from the Thazeattebin area, and that it would now be necessary for the 81st Division to capture Myohaung itself. Christmas was therefore no holiday. The weather by now was bitterly cold at night and the troops were constantly subjected to shelling to which there was practically no reply. In addition the Christmas supplies were late, and there was a lot of work to be done consolidating the westward bend of the Yau Chaung before the final push to the south.

In all this period there were frequent patrol clashes with the Japs, who kept probing eastwards over the ridge which divided the opposing forces, but they were always in our favour. The Sierra Leone Regiment had secured a vital pass by capturing Point 887, and now, almost immediately on our arrival, we were detailed to secure Point 619, about two miles to the south. The action fought by Lt. Rother's patrol, which is described by himself in Appendix . . . . . . , was typical of the type of action going on at this time.

South of Naleik, and of the Yau Chaung bend, the ridges continued in the same formation towards Myohaung. The advance could be continued in a valley among the hills, if the Japs allowed it, but now it was in the short Naleik Chaung, which flowed northwards instead of south. This chaung petered out at a saddle about half a mile north of the village of Angyaung, and over the saddle yet another stream took the running to Ma Kyaze. But all the time as the advance moved southward, the broad ridge which had screened us from the Kyauktaw plain grew ever narrower, so that the task for the defenders was made progressively more easy. Time was running short for us. At Ma Kyaze, the narrowest point of the ridge, unless we were to break east once more into the hills, we were likely to find our most difficult problem.

In the meantime any further advance past Naleik was not going to be feasible unless the high ground south of it was in our hands, and the days between Christmas and the New Year were spent in continuous movement with this object in view. Using Point 619 as a base, the Battalion infiltrated gradually across the Yau Chaung with minor but fierce engagements taking place every day. At the same time the 8th Gold Coast were pushing southwards along the high ground overlooking the Naleik Chaung.

It was not easy going. About four miles to the southwest of Point 619 lay a ridge which came to be known as the "Westdown Feature", flanking the motor road which ran under the other side of it, and in the whole area between, the enemy were in some strength. They also had the majority of their guns there. The Jap was therefore in a very **powerful** position to counter attack, which made it essential that we bit off nothing more than we could chew.

The difficulty of dealing in any other way with Westdown brought us the heaviest air support that we had yet experienced on either campaign. Quite early in the morning of December 29th, moving majestically in tight formation, we watched the squadrons of Mitchells fly slowly and deliberately up the length of the ridge with the dust of the bomb bursts spouting and spreading behind them, while the atmosphere rumbled and the ground shook beneath our own feet. In the afternoon a second saturation raid was delivered, and from their grand stand view up among the hills the Africans forgot the moment, dropped their weapons and danced and cheered. They had never seen anything quite like it before.

Later, when the ridge was occupied, though we found the biggest dump that had yet been discovered, there was but one lonely disconsolate Jap remaining.

As the hills overlooking the Yau Chaung were secured, 6th Brigade once more began to advance, this time along the valley of the Naleik Chaung. The saddle at Angyaung was quickly secured but at Ma Kyaze, as might have been expected, the way was barred and the enemy were found to be in strength on what came to be known as "Starfish" overlooking it. In spite of air support and the limited help afforded by the mountain battery, it was not possible to shift them. There were no tanks, and it was the same old story. The Japs held the ridge tops; the slopes were too steep and the only feasible approaches were cleverly blocked by heavy machine gun fire. By this time too, of course, their artillery was on to every move, and for the first time the Japs were also getting reasonably heavy support from their own mortars. If the time factor had been less urgent, it would have been possible to by-pass to the east, but now this area had become particularly broken, and the bend of the Lemro had narrowed the manoeuvrable area to a matter of about four miles.

So the responsibility for further progress once more shifted to 5th Brigade. The leading elements were quickly ordered to close up on to the high ground north west of Ma Kyaze, and a detachment was sent to "Westdown", there to cover the construction of a fighter air strip, which could supply almost immediate support in the event of opposition. This was quite a bold move, considering that the field lay within six miles of the foremost troops in an area where no such thing as a "Line" existed.

The plan now was for two battalions to outflank "Starfish" from the west. 5th Gold Coast were to secure Point 564, which lay about three miles due south of the enemy position; 8th Gold Coast were to make a far longer and wider sweep, to come in at the Thingyittaw Pagoda, a further three miles south, from which they could cover the Thazeattebin road and block one of the Japanese lines of withdrawal.

It is not right to criticize any plan where all the facts which were known at the time are still not available, but at least it seemed as if an error was made here.

If it could be assumed that the Pagoda might be captured, the ground-objective was practically assured, for between it and Myohaung there was no satisfactory area from which a successful defensive action could be maintained. Above Myohaung, the long ridge petered out, and for two or three miles to the north the hills were formless and cut up, just as a wave is breaking on the shore. The area of the Pagoda and the ground running due east from it was the point at which the wave was about to break. There was therefore really but one requirement - to secure the *whole of this area,* and only then to draw the net tight.

A pause here to glance at the map is informative, and even though the map may be far from accurate, the possibility of what might have been done is interesting.

In the first place then, the dominating influence of the Pagoda is obvious, though the little hill features just to the south west of it are perhaps even more important. The Pagoda might be the key to any attempted block, but the smaller hills are actually those which command the road. Turning east, and only a mile and a half away, there is the track over a saddle, running south from Ma Kyaze, and above it Point 459 and the spur running east to Hnetgaung - two further enemy lines of withdrawal. Finally, to the north, there is the village of Kretsin, which covers the only other constructed track along which the enemy might slip away across the Lemro. It seems possible that if these had been blocked the enemy might really have been brought to battle and mainly destroyed to the north of Myohaung.

The move to Kretsin should not have been difficult, particularly in view of the fact that the approaches to "Starfish" were narrow and that large numbers of troops could not be employed in frontal attack. The movement of two battalions, however, to the Pagoda and Point 459 would have been by no means so simple. It meant a wide flank march through the paddy area, where cover was very scanty and where tidal chaungs obstructed all the way. The Jap artillery was intact, and casualties - if the move were discovered - might have been very heavy indeed. Yet there were many "yets" to this question. If the prize was worth-while, was it not worth the possible risk to do this? If one battalion could do it, could not two? and if the enemy artillery opened up by day, was not the air force there to deal with it? Finally if secrecy was the factor, would not the mere revelation of the move have caused the enemy to alter his dispositions to meet it? There is no value in carrying the supposition further, but the fact that the enemy eventually escaped almost intact, at least gives it some interest.

The move to capture Point 564 was not one that was appreciated by the company commanders in 5th Gold Coast. Their route lay across the chaung running west from Ma Kyaze, and then continued along the bottom of the foothills of the main ridge. The distance would be some five miles, taking a straight line, and for the greater part of the way they knew that the enemy would be poised above and behind them, watching every movement. It was truly to be a case of running the gauntlet.

However on January 15th the battalion started off on the attempt. The plan was for "A" Company to cover three bounds as far as Melaung, and then for "B" and "C" to pass through, making independently for the ridge tops by routes which could only be reconnoitred from air photographs. After that the remainder of the battalion would build up on Point 564. The column had been stripped of all unnecessary headloaders, who were left behind in charge of the quartermaster, and apart from having the mountain battery at call, the C.O. would also get fighter-bomber support from the airstrip now at "Westdown". Large orange and gold umbrellas were issued to the forward troops so that they could be identified in their forward positions by the aircraft.

Before dawn the leading company disappeared quietly out of the battalion position and then, quite soon after it was light, bombers flew high over the column and engaged the ridge south of "Starfish" in addition to the foothills which patrols had found occupied a day or two before. As the main body crossed the chaung flowing west from Ma Kyaze, they could hear 1st Sierra Leone opening up their own attack with a mortar concentration high up on the left. An hour later a second wave of Mediums flew down the ridge to bombard Point 425, but on these steep, narrow, chaung scarred hills the value was more majestic than effective. After each strike the leading troops moved forward once again, maintaining their position a thousand yards behind the bomb line.

The battalion was now advancing practically in single file along a thin line of scrub which was the only available piece of cover running parallel with the hills. There were several places on the route which were exposed to observation from the ridge; the cattle tracks were overgrown and difficult to negotiate, even for men without headloads, and several deep, muddy chaungs made it a continual struggle to move steadily forward. Progress was therefore very slow. No risks could be taken. And all the time single aircraft sped overhead, straffing the villages to the south of us, while the 3.7s could be heard from Westdown firing into the same area.

At 1800 hours, far later than had been hoped, "A" Company contacted the enemy on a little line of hills roughly parallel with the ridge and drove them off the second of them by the use of their mortars. But the leading platoon now found that the enemy were holding the next behind it, and had broken the foot-bridge which crossed a deep tidal chaung running in front of it.

The situation was an unpleasant one. The battalion was strung out behind along a narrow line of scrub with another deep chaung on its right and open paddy beyond, with its front blocked and covered, and with another stretch of open paddy across to the foothills. There was clearly no room for manoeuvre, and the whole narrow area presented a first class target for the enemy artillery with its O.Ps obviously on the ridge tops overlooking us. In addition it would soon be dark and there was still more than two miles to the objective.

Brigade orders had been to go into close harbour by 1600 hours, but they may have scarcely realized the incredible slowness of an advance - to all intents - along a narrow defile. At any rate, in spite of the time, a last attempt was made to dislodge the Japs before night fell. A patrol of "A" Company tried to work round the flank but it was heavily grenaded from above while bogged in the mud of the chaung, and could not make any progress. In any case the cover was so narrow in this area that no further attempt could possibly succeed in daylight. Further attempt might have been made, but just then "B" Company made contact with the Japs at the foot of the ridge to the north-east, so it became essential to consolidate at once before darkness spread confusion.

"B" Company was immediately ordered to secure the spurs on which they had made contact, while the remainder of the battalion set to work to dig itself in as securely as it could, more or less where they were already. It was dangerous to stay at all, and the Japs lost the opportunity of a lifetime. They energetically opposed "B" Company's efforts to get a foothole on their vital spur, and counter-attacked vigorously, but the position was gained nevertheless. An attempt by "C" Company to infiltrate a platoon from Point 561 during the night was foiled by their watchfulness. The battalion area was also subjected to artillery and mortar fire, but it was not very concentrated and the attack we feared never materialized.

When dawn came the enemy again attacked "B" Company but were driven off, and now because the prospect of forcing the obstacle in front seemed hopeless in face of increasing opposition, and because the 8th Gold Coast had been successful in reaching Thingyittaw Pagoda, the battalion was ordered to break away in to the foothills to the north.

The position there was not much better. It was closely overlooked by enemy post, still intact, facing 6th Brigade, and there was fierce sporadic fighting for the next two days. First a platoon of "C" Company was heavily attacked by a force twice its numbers while attempting to in-filtrate to a feature further south. Then the battalion area was subjected to the heaviest night's shelling which it had yet experienced, finally an attack by "D" Company was driven back after severe casualties, particularly among the Europeans - an action in which an African Sergeant acquitted himself brilliantly in command of two platoon.

The shelling scored direct hits on the battalion Command Post and on the rum ration, but there were practically no casualties, for apart from being most efficient diggers by now, the Africans had learnt to provide themselves with head-cover as well in a space of time far inside the capabilities of nearly any other troop. Though it was only as thick as a man's arm, it was sufficient to withstand a direct hit by a Japanese shell.

All this activity, however, was apparently the final gesture of defiance of a retreating enemy. Evidently the capture of the Pagoda had taken immediate effect, for at the time when "D" Company were being fiercely repulsed a strong patrol led by Captain Benson was moving south along the paddy without opposition, and they managed to establish themselves in the villages south-east of Auk Thagan.

Thereafter things moved with increasing momentum. On the day after "D" Company's attack the position was found clear by "A" Company. From the paddy, Captain Benson had worked up onto the ridge and found it clear. 6th Brigade was also on the move. Though by night, and sometimes by day, the Japs artillery continued to harass the river crossings and movement in the plain, it was obvious that their positions had crumbled and that they were pulling out.

The 82nd Division now made contact with the 81st some miles to the west of Myohaung. While our own troops moved rapidly across the hills to cut off the Japanese crossing the Lemro, their leading elements began a wider pincer movement to the north and south of the town.

But it was too late. The opportunity which perhaps could have been created between the Pagoda and Hnetgaung had not been seized, and operating on interior lines the enemy were breaking into small parties to avoid our grasp. They *had* actually used the track near Hnetgaung to evacuate the majority of their force at "Starfish". Up till the 25th January there were frequent small actions between our advanced troops and the Japanese rear parties, but that afternoon, on the banks of the Lemro, the last Japs were chased out of the village of Sinogyi and "C" Company, report their position, discovered that theirs were the last shots to be fired by the battalion.

So Myohaung was taken, and the second Kaladan campaign was at an end. Thereafter the 82nd West African Division took up the running, and we, without elation, but with a sense of satisfaction at a job completed, waited to be flown out by the Dakotas which alone had enabled us to reach the town in this dusty plain, and to march through those green hills whose broken outlines and hot, tangled undergrowth had also - curiously enough - been such a factor in our success.

CHAPTER XV

REFLECTION

THE capture of Myohaung hastened the Jap domination of the Arakan to its speedy conclusion a few weeks later. From small beginnings - that is the securing of 15th Corps' left flank - our operations had quickly developed until we, in fact, were playing the major part in the whole operation. That at least was what Lord Louis Mountbatten had given us to understand when he flew in to see us after it was all over.

"Gentlemen", he told us. "I have to thank *you* for the capture of Akyab". If this was just necessary praise, at least it was a brief and pleasant way of telling us how well we had done. By getting astride his main escape route from the coastal area, we had compelled the Japanese to break up their force into small parties in their attempts to break out over the rough mountain tracks to the south - east. The subsequent landings at Ramree and Cheduba, and the cutting of the southern escape route at Kangaw completed the disruption, and put an end once for all to the last threat to the Indian frontier.

Physically, the second campaign had been much easier than the first, though it was only easy in comparison to it. There was nothing in it to compare with the sustained rush southwards to Kyauktaw and Apaukwa, followed by that immediate and equally rapid withdrawal; and then again by that very arduous march out of the Kaladan into the valley of the Kalapanzin. It was also shorter by two months than the first campaign and, after Myohaung, there is no doubt that the division could have fought on for a good deal longer, if need be. These remarks apply more to the 5th Brigade however, because it should be remembered that the 6th were employed actively on the Burma frontier almost immediately following First Kaladan, and had remained there, living in the jungle throughout the monsoon, until the second series of operations were begun.

It would not be fair to compare the two sets of operations, because the factors operating were so different. In the first campaign we were untrained - very green, at least - and without experience of the jungle. The lessons of General Wingate's expedition had not reached us, and we were therefore as much pioneers as were his raiders. Our methods of supply and our equipment were still very much experimental. And though there was great loyalty between officer and man, and even affection, there was not the same confidence as was born later after great labour and hard experiences shared. Finally the enemy in December 1943 was still a victorious enemy, who had yet to come within an ace of success at Imphal and only then to realize that the tide had turned, as he was swept slowly back to the Irrawaddy. Nevertheless, the interest in comparison compels one to make it.

In the first campaign the attempt was made to use a limited amount of transport for the artillery, the signals and for formation staffs, and the result was failure. With only two brigades in the division, there was an inevitable lack of compactness and therefore of security, and if the enemy had acted with greater vigour and intelligence there might well have been serious consequences. Limited in manoeuvre by the necessity of roads, it was necessary to make our movements at a speed almost beyond our capacity in order to achieve surprise. By the second campaign we had already learnt - provided there was continuous air supply - that a large force of African troops could manage far better without any transport at all, and in spite of a twenty percent cut in ammunition and personal equipment off the original very light scale. It was then possible to surmount almost any obstacle at considerable speed, and surprise for the Jap was the order of the day. On the other hand the advantage was not pressed too far. A high reserve of physical energy was regarded of being quite as important as a reserve of material, so that the maximum march aimed at was seldom more than eight miles a day. We had learnt, to our cost, that physical reserves - once expended - were extremely difficult to regain.

Apart from shorter marches, the intervals between one move and another were on the whole longer, which allowed for a greater number of supply drops. This meant, on the second campaign, that only two to three days rations had to be carried on the man in comparison with four to five days on the first, when in actual fact a large part of the ration had normally to be thrown away to relieve the weight carried.

That morale was higher at our second attempt was only to be expected. Nobody any longer overestimated the Jap as they had, before all the well-meaning propaganda had been debunked in action ; and the Africans and Europeans had developed a greater confidence and trust in each other. Both had learnt their own limitations. The African relied on his officers for imagination and foresight, for quick appraisal of a situation and clear orders ; the European, to rely far more on the African's instinct for danger, and to trust much more his amazing powers of hearing and observation. We had all learnt that speed in a jungle battle was purely relative and that, if anything it was to be regarded as a tactical danger. There were other much more important requirements : to acquire a complete knowledge of the ground before you struck ; to maintain control if possible, but to leave room for initiative where the unexpected is so common placed; to allow time, and more time, in which to ensure that nothing can go wrong.

We had learnt that the Jap had his tricks, but never thought them out spontaneously. Over a period of years, perhaps, they had been perfected and assiduously learnt, but he was quite unable to produce new methods. We were sure of our own weapons and our ability to select the right ground for defence, and we could be almost equally certain that that would be the enemy's selected line of approach, and his objective; and that he would continue to attack it until utterly exhausted.

All these things, and very many more, we had been forced to learn in First Kaladan by practical, and sometimes bitter experience.

The greatest difficulty in both campaigns was that of communication at the lower levels. The No. 22 Set made it perfectly easy between Battalion and Brigade, but the No. 48 Set, issued to companies was too bulky to carry about at close quarters on steep slopes during an action.

Thus it often came about that a company commander had to leave his forward platoons in order to send a message to battalion headquarters, or was forced to continue his battle leaving them in the dark. The sets were often unreliable among the steep, tree-clad slopes which tended to screen transmission, and in the humid atmosphere we worked in. Further training helped, and also a much more liberal use of 'line', but that was not enough.

The real problem was not so much that a company commander could not report to his C. O., but that he himself could obtain little accurate data to report. Let him once launch his platoons into action and they at once disappear. Two hundred yards away on his left, perhaps - up above him - he can hear one of his platoons in action; there is silence from the other, somewhere down the hill on his right. He may make for one or the other, but he knows quite well it will take fully half an hour to get from one *to* the other. In the meantime the emphasis of the battle may swing, and in a matter of minutes, swing back again. It can be seen that in using runners he was faced with the same difficulties, receiving no more than a late, hurried, and second-hand picture of the situation. The "walkie-talkie", therefore, issued right down to platoons, was really essential to any well co-ordinated attack in this type of country, and it was one of the few things we were without.

In both campaigns the R. A. F. gave us excellent support, but if there were certainly less aircraft available in the first there was also, perhaps, a disposition only to make use of air support when other methods failed. Later it became almost routine, for any position which the enemy was holding to be subjected to preliminary bombing and strafing from the air. The Japs hated this form of attack, and if it was not always essential for the capture of a position, it must have exercised a cumulative effect on his morale, while the attacks were particularly heartening overtures for African troops. The enemy were quick to recognise the preliminaries to an air attack, and as time went on they showed less and less disposition to accept it.

We were very grateful to the R. A. F. Much time and many casualties were undoubtedly saved as a result of their support, but we sometimes felt that they were inclined to be to dogmatic about the whole procedure. "Give us the extent and nature of the target", they would say, "and *we* will decide the force required for it." We were rather more conscious of our own liability for error. "O. K. by us," we felt. "But why not double it for luck, if you *have* the aircraft?"
This they did not want to do.

But we knew how easy it was to be a little wrong in a country where visibility was zero. You bump the enemy and know he's there. But where are *you*? It is not possible to climb a piece of bamboo to take your bearings, and when you get back to a point of vantage .... Was it there? Or there? Everything is so much the same. Our maps were not always accurate, and a smoke bomb was not certain to hit the centre of the area on these razor - backs or small pimples where the Japs always had their positions. Though the R. A. F. had many successes, we felt that the principle if possible should always be extravagance rather than nicety of calculation.

Finally, in the second campaign, we experienced the advantage of all the little things which one learns, and goes on learning, so long as fighting continues. To travel light was both necessary *and* comfortable, once you learnt how. A little over twenty pounds was the extent of each man's kit, and it was enough. The groundsheet, fitted into a hollow in the ground, gave us our daily bath; the bulk of the mosquito net could be cut away until it stood only a few inches above one's head; never more than a single pair of boots was carried, nor more than a single change of clothing. Bamboo leaves made a matress, and the haversack a good pillow. There were but two to three hurricane lamps in the whole battalion. The doctor carried all his medical equipments in four small loads; magazine boxes were discarded for haversacks, and pick heads, helves and shovels were pared down to the minimum of wood and metal.

Yet with all our cuts and experiments, a sensible, practical outlook was maintained. "There must be a standard to base ourselves on," the General would say. "But if you have a particular fad you can have it". There were no absolute rules.

Some units, for instance, always carried bren tripos, whereas we dispensed with them in order to carry more signal wire. Others insisted that all Africans should wear boots, but we were permitted to dispose of them in the interests of speed and silence. Instead, we made every man carry at least one grenade-corporal, C.O. or cook -in order to maintain the greatest possible reserve. There was also a sensible attitude as regards the matter of equality of effort, and it caused no heart-burnings and undoubtedly paid in the long run. Recognising the superiority of the African in load carrying, and the necessary activity and responsibility of the European, no effort was made to ensure equal loads, and Europeans did not carry their packs but gave them to their boys.

Our more sedate pace in the second campaign ensured a higher physical tone than on the first, but as in all tropical campaigns the losses on account of sickness were always high. We quickly learnt the deadliness of untreated water, and the absolute necessity of salt and Vitamin C; but the toll typhus, small-pox, malaria and septic sores was a constant drain. They could be curbed but never eradicated.

Battle casualties, as the Appendix shows, were never high, but it was necessary to ensure this as far as possible because of the difficulty of getting reinforcements.

There was nothing very spectacular about either of the Kaladan campaigns; no defeats, nor victories which would appeal to the public imagination. The forces employed on either side were comparatively small, and their weapons only the basic weapons of the infantry soldier. Yet the operations played their part in the hard slogging which eventually broke down the Japanese power in Burma.

The early battles in Arakan stemmed the enemy's advance along the easiest route into India, including the complicated area around which would have caused administrative chaos if it had been lost. The battles later on demoralized the Japs, causing them many thousands of casualties, and later drew off the extra forces which might have been the decisive factor in the plains of Imphal. It was in these last that the 81st West African Division played its part.

If the actions the West Africans fought were shorter and less bloody than some of those on other fronts, they were fiercely contested nonetheless. It is probably because they were out-manoeuvred at every step that the Japanese were so seldom able to stand and make a fight. They were eventually outmatched in tactics, in jungle craft, and almost in physical endurance ; and it was in this physical aspect that the Division has, perhaps, reason to be most proud. The very conception of West African Way was bold in face of the limited time available and the appalling nature of the country it had to cross. The very discovery of a trace which was usable was something of a feat in itself, and the way in which its seventy odd miles was completed in three weeks with only pick, dynamite and shovel, was an achievement. The marches we followed, and the constant manoeuvring and fighting among the wild hills on the Burma border approached, at times, the limits of human endurance.

The part played by the African soldier in these struggles, I hope, will not be quickly forgotten. It was valuable and most generous given. We, who were with them - if our achievements were not epic - at least will always be proud of the task that was done. But we will be prouder still of the unit we had helped to knit together and of our patient African troops, who grasped so little of the war's true meaning - of their endurance, their humour, their loyalty and true courage.

Appendix "D"

MILEAGES COVERED BY 5TH GOLD COAST REGT.

1st. CAMPAIGN.

Chiringa	-	Balaing (West African Way)	85
Balaing	-	Dokang	10
Dokang	-	Leingkine	7
Leingkine	-	Konwei	15
Konwei	-	Themawa	7½
Themawa	-	Natarraingyaung	6½
Nat.	-	Kammang	3
Kammang	-	Bunwa	10
Bunwa	-	Mindanywa	11
Min.	-	Point 13	2
Point 13	-	Minthazeik	11
Minthazeik, moves in vicinity			15
Minthazeik	-	"Cow's Corner"	10½
C. C.	-	Kwingi North	7
K. W.	-	Wabyan	5
Wabyan	-	Sabaseik	5
Sabaseik	-	Daleingdaung	2
Dal.	-	Lasaung	4½
Lasaung	-	Ngame	5½
Ngame	-	Kyauktan	6
Kyauktan	-	Kaladan	6
Kaladan	-	Kammang	5
Kammang	-	Yadaung	17
Yadaung	-	Wagai	10
Wagai	-	Talubya	12
Talubya	-	Point 77	12
Pt. 77	-	Letpanywa	13½
Let.	-	Point 433	5½
Pt. 433	-	"Long Ridge"	4
L. Ridge	-	Taung Bazaar	6
T. Bazaar	-	Bawli Bazaar	20
			339½

Notes.

1. The above are map mileages.
2. Allowance for innumerable bends in native tracks - 1/5 -   66 miles.
3. Allowance for peculiarly hilly country   42 ,,

   Total   447 miles.

4. Patrol leaders probably did an extra 10 miles a week for 6 months - 240

   Total   687 miles.

2ND CAMPAIGN.

The map mileage in this campaign was about 220 miles. Making the same allowances as in 2 and 3 above the extra distance would be about 71 miles. This would make a grand total of

1078 miles.

Patrol leaders who went through both campaigns probably did more than this, entirely on foot, mostly over hills which must be nearly the steepest, on the average, in the world.

The total distance on metalled roads must have been less than 20 miles.

Appendix 'E'

BRITISH CASUALTIES - 1st CAMPAIGN.

	European	African
Killed	25	162
Wounded	101	726
Missing	7	150
Total	133	1038

ESTIMATED JAPANESE CASUALTIES.

55 Div. Cavalry	Strength	700	Casualties	570
Matsuo Butai	,,	600	,,	550
III Regiment	,,	500	,,	360
J. I. F. & I. N. A.	,,	300	,,	80

Note.
Casualties for the second campaign not yet available.

5th Bn. GOLD COAST REGIMENT

	European	African
Killed	5	37
Wounded	16	18
Missing	3	185

Appendix "F"

EXTRACTS OF CITATIONS OF AFRICAN AWARDS

Sgt. Dogo Yerwa - Awarded D.C.M.

ON the night of 15/16 Dec. 1945 at Tinma West Sgt. Dogo Yerwa was commanding the forward platoon of "A" Company astride a ridge ... At 1915 hours his position was attacked by at least a company of the enemy with considerable artillery support. The attack was pressed home with the utmost determination for seven hours without respite. The full force of the attack fell on Sgt. Yerwa's platoon, the ridge being too narrow to allow reserves to do anything but pass ammunition. Early in the action he was wounded by grenade splinters ... Throughout 7 hours of fighting he went from section to section controlling the fire and himself firing rifle grenades from the hip. His task was the more difficult as two section commanders and 14 men were wounded. Only when severely wounded himself at the end of the action was he evacuated. 16 enemy bodies were found in and about his platoon.

Sgt. Hassan Bazabarimi—Awarded D.C.M.

On 15 Jan. 1945 near Teinnyo, during operations to clear the foothills Sgt. Hassan Bazabarimi was platoon sergeant of a platoon sent to reinforce a section patrol, which had occupied an enemy position on a spur, on which it was intended to build up a company. On arrival it was found that the section had been heavily attacked and forced to withdraw. At the same time the British Sergeant commanding the platoon was wounded and the 2 i/c of the company, who was in charge of the operation, was killed. The enemy were pressing in increasing strength. Sgt. Hassan Bazabarimi took command and organized his platoon to cover the withdrawal of the section which had lost both of its N.C.Os, and personally led the party which recovered the body of the 2 i/c and brought out all the wounded under heavy fire. He then established his platoon on the end of a spur and held the position against repeated attacks for two hours, thus allowing the company to build up behind him. During the night 15/16 Jan. 1945 the position was shelled and mortared and at dawn, after further mortaring, the enemy attacked ... The attack was beaten off without loss.

Later when the company was withdrawn, Sgt. Hassan ... commanded the rear guard with skill in the face of opposition. ......

Sgt. Sidiki Moshi - Awarded D.C.M.

On 17 Jan. 1945 near Teinnyo ... Sgt. Sidkii Mosh was platoon sergeant ... during an attack on a strongly held enemy position on a steep ridge. The platoon commander was wounded and Sgt. Sidiki took command, leading the platoon towards the objective in the face of determined resistance. The company came under heavy mortar and machine gunfire and suffered heavy casualties, including four out of five Europeans, but (he) continued to press forward with great determination in an attempt to complete the final assault. It became evident, however, that the position had become untenable. Casualties were mounting and many wounded were lying exposed in front of the enemy, and orders were issued to withdraw. At this point Sgt. Sidiki also took command of No. 12 Platoon ... Not until all except one man had been brought out did he start the withdrawal, in which he exercised perfect control of both platoons.

.... it was entirely due to his magnificent example and skilful leadership that the casualties were evacuated and the two platoons successfully extricated from an awkward situation.

OTHER AFRICAN AWARDS.

Military Medals	11.
B. E. M.	1
Mentions in Despatches	17

In addition there was an unofficial badge for brave or distinguished conduct awarded to many of the African troops. This was allowed to be worn in an active theatre of operations. It consisted of a plain bar of scarlet cloth, worn just below the right shoulder. The Africans were very proud of it, and it did a lot to raise the morale of the unit.

Some of the awards of the M. M. were for extremely brave and resourceful actions, but it would take too long to record them here.

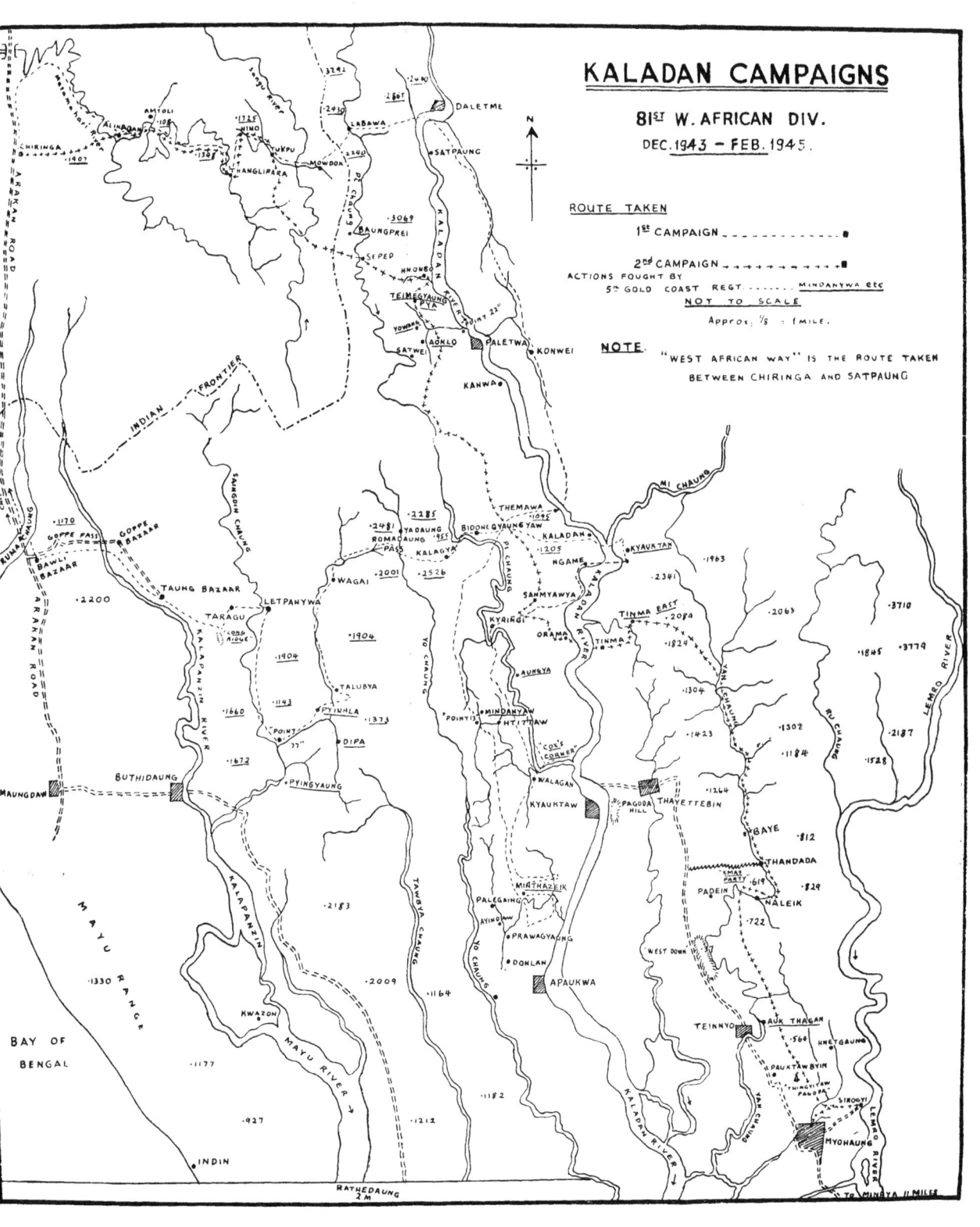

www.ingramcontent.com/pod-product-compliance
Ingram Content Group UK Ltd.
Pitfield, Milton Keynes, MK11 3LW, UK
UKHW051652180426
11947UKWH00021B/1921